Beyond the Gold Watch

Beyond the Gold Watch

Living in Retirement

Deborah V. Gross

Westminster John Knox Press
Louisville, Kentucky

Book and cover design by Drew Stevens
Cover illustration by Julius Friedman. Used with permission.

First edition

This book is printed on acid-free paper that meets the American National Standards Institute Z39.48 standard. ♾

Published by Westminster John Knox Press
Louisville, Kentucky

PRINTED IN THE UNITED STATES OF AMERICA
9 8 7 6 5 4 3 2 1

Library of Congress Cataloging-in-Publication Data

Gross, Deborah V., date.
    Beyond the gold watch : living in retirement / Deborah V. Gross. —
1st ed.
        p.   cm.
    Includes bibliographical references.
    ISBN 0-664-25449-7 (alk. paper)
    1. Retirement—United States.   2. Retirees—United States—Life
skills guides.   I. Title.
HQ1063.2.U6G76   1994
306.3'8—dc20   93-44993

In loving memory of
Irene and W. J. Gross

Contents

Introduction

Mr. Abernathy,* an administrative assistant for a large corporation, did not understand or plan for his life after retirement. When he was fifty-nine, his wife died. Mr. Abernathy retired "on schedule" at age sixty-five, having made no preparations other than going over the pension plan with his personnel manager. He retired to an empty house.

Mrs. Abernathy had always been the social organizer for the couple. He had no activities or interests that were not work related. Over the next ten years, Mr. Abernathy became more and more withdrawn. He had enough money to live on and his physical health was good. But his life was emotionally empty, devoid of people and purpose. He became severely depressed, and he began to focus on his physical health, going from doctor to doctor with many different symptoms in an almost continuous state of panic. He was finally hospitalized for psychiatric treatment. There he expressed his deep loneliness and hopelessness, and he talked about how he had never really visualized himself as retired. He wondered if death would have been more humane.

This sad story might have been different had Mr. Abernathy realized that his life was more than his work. He might have planned for the changes that came with retirement, age, and loss. He might not have retired at all! But these options did not occur to him and he made no plans. Yes, loss and some kinds of illness are more common in later

*All names and historical details have been altered to protect the privacy of those involved.

life. Yes, some of these changes are simply a matter of luck and no one has control over them. But *you* can maximize your life after retirement by planning for it.

Society thinks of older people as unproductive and finished. At best, the attitude is one of indulgent tolerance, and at worst, of blatant discrimination. How many stereotypes do you recognize in the following myth list?

Myth List

Old people are	sick	senile
	deaf	blind
	stupid	weak
	passive	set in their ways
	all alike	hopeless
	ugly	complainers
	dependent	broken of body
	debilitated	dull of mind
	in nursing homes	lonely
Old people cannot	learn and change	benefit from medical
	contribute much	or psychiatric care
	to society	work effectively
Old people should	always retire and	accept unfairness
	be happy about it	with a beneficent
	move aside for the	smile of wisdom
	young	
Old people should not	take risks	go to school
	work for a living	have sex

How do these myths about aging relate to retirement? Retirement in our society puts you in a box labeled *old* (or *senior citizen, golden ager, elderly,* or even *retiree*). *Old* is then equated with sickness and senility, and the box (with you in it) is placed neatly on a shelf. Society says: All old people are sick and worthless, all retired people are old, and therefore all retired people are sick and worthless. This is nonsense. But if you believe it, you might act on it (or, worse yet, let it act on you) and fail to get the most out of your later life.

This book is not about the one true road to happiness and health, nor is it a prescription for panacea in old age. Regardless of age, some people adjust to change better than others. Some people do not adjust well to later life. But neither retirement nor the aging process itself is to blame. People fail to adjust either because they did not adequately prepare, or because the problems they face outstrip the resources they can muster to deal with them.

The fact is that with knowledge and planning you can minimize your problems, maximize your resources, and facilitate your adjustment to later life. The goals of this book are to give you accurate information and to help you plan for a happy and fulfilling time in your life.

You need information to fight the confusion about retirement and aging and to arm yourself against ignorance. You have to know yourself and your situation, you must anticipate and take steps to prevent or solve potential problems. Naturally, there is no way to shield yourself against every sling and arrow, but that is no reason to shed your common sense altogether and pretend you can't predict and prepare for some of them. Learning and planning are skills. You can do both to get the most out of your later life if you are willing to ignore that foolishness about old dogs and new tricks.

Who Can Use This Book?

This book can help you if:
1. You're thinking about retirement but haven't decided when and how.
2. You're anxious about retiring or getting older.
3. You already have retired but have not adjusted satisfactorily. You want some new ideas.
4. You don't plan to retire but want to make some contingency plans in case you change your mind later.
5. You don't plan to retire, but you do want to learn ways to get more from your later life.
6. You're trying to help someone else deal with the changes of later life.

When Should You Start Planning?

The earlier you start planning, the better. You can use the principles outlined in this book to start making changes in your life at any time, including well after you actually have retired. *Ideally, though, you should begin the process at least a year before you make any changes in your work status.* To start later is to risk your control of the problems you may find.

How to Use the Book to Make Your Plan

The book will guide you through the planning process step by step. There are worksheets and checklists to help you. Give yourself as much time as you need to complete each of the steps. If you get frustrated, take a break and come back to it later. The issues are detailed and interrelated. You will be thinking new thoughts and arranging old ones in new ways. The investment of extra time and effort can only help you.

Forget all the old rules against writing in books. If I could walk around the "class," I would hope to see notes and ideas scribbled in the margins of every page. This is a *working* book. It should stir your imagination, and you should write down thoughts as they come to you.

Calvin Coolidge once said that "we cannot do everything at once, but we can do something at once." Retirement planning can be discouragingly complex, but don't wait. *Don't assume that things will work out in the end.* Planning will give you a better chance of making your later life rewarding. Remember that you are planning for a part of your life, not a preamble to death. There is no eleventh commandment that says thou shalt retire at age sixty-five and park thyself in the rocking chair thereafter. On the other hand, there is no commandment that says thou shalt *not* do this either. That's the beauty of it; the choice is yours.

Part 1

Facts

1 Why You Need to Plan

It wasn't raining when Noah built the ark.
—*Howard Ruff*

Let's say that you are a sixty-year-old man, with a wife, three grown children, and a Labrador retriever named Cashew. You have worked for a large firm for more than twenty-eight years. You have a comfortable income, a couple of individual retirement accounts (IRAs), a house in the suburbs, and a cabin on a lake near the city where you live. You are trying to decide whether to retire. You need to talk to your family and friends, decide where you will live, and figure out how to make the most of your financial, physical, and mental resources. What will you do should any of these fail you? How will you spend your time? Will you be satisfied? Is your wife prepared to cope with everyday matters if she loses you? How would you manage if you lost her? People sometimes don't get very far in planning for retirement and later life because the number and diversity of things to be considered quickly bring on a kind of mental paralysis.

Human beings plan for three general reasons: to make good things happen, to keep bad things from happening, and to feel involved and in control. In preparing for retirement and later life, you want to decrease your risk of adjusting poorly and maximize your physical, psychological, and social resources. You want to feel that you are in control of things, that you have options in your life, and that you are not simply at the mercy of circumstances.

Most people who say they have adjusted well to retirement and later life have one thing in common: They've planned for it. Retirement can serve as a "trigger" to get you started planning for later life,[1] but the planning itself has a positive effect.[2] Health, enough money,

3

and good relationships also help, but when these things are factored out of the equation, the positive effect of planning remains.

All right, you may say, planning is a good idea in general. But retirement and getting older are so commonplace. Do I really need to make a special effort to prepare for them? The answer is yes, and the reason is this: Neither society nor the workplace is going to help you much in planning for satisfaction at this time in your life.

In fact, only one in ten American workers has access to any kind of retirement planning at all, and only a small proportion of this 10 percent learns about anything more than the pension plan.[3] Organizations of various types outside the workplace offer general information about aging, but these are not usually individualized. This is especially unfortunate, because the "one size fits all" concept is nowhere less useful than in later life.

So much for the workplace. What about society? In earlier life, you were prepared ahead of time for the roles you would play later. Maybe you remember playing "house" as a child, or pretending to be a fire fighter, doctor, or basketball star? Perhaps you "courted" your spouse before marriage, or you worked at several different jobs before settling into your current occupation.

Contrast that kind of social preparation with the messages you get in our culture about being an older person. Remember the *Myth List*? These messages are usually confusing and sometimes dangerously stereotypical. You are on your own!

There can be some advantages, however. Later life differs from earlier life in that what you do becomes governed less by the norms and standards of society and more by your own desires. You can turn this to your own benefit, but you need a plan—a customized blueprint—to make the most of this time in your life. What follows is a list of what you can expect to gain for the planning efforts.

Knowing What to Expect— Decreased Anxiety

Fear of the unknown is common and debilitating. Needless anxiety can interfere with your ability to adjust and cope with problems. If, for example, you believe that retirement causes mental and physical decline, you may feel helpless and give up before you start. Having the facts, making decisions, and planning effectively for later life will help you feel confident and in control. Ms. Nelson is an example of how this can work. As manager of a large chain of department stores, she had devoted her life to her work. She had never married, and most of her social life revolved around the business. She was hospitalized at age sixty for a mild heart attack, and during her recovery she began to think about her life. She had not really thought about retirement before, nor about what the aging process meant to her. She took a course titled "Issues in Aging" at a local university, and she began to realize that there were underdeveloped areas in her life.

Ms. Nelson decided that, while she enjoyed her work and did not want to retire completely, she did want to try something new. Over the next few years, she began to cut back her hours at work and pursue other interests. A veteran of many business trips, she still enjoyed travel. She incorporated learning new languages and cultures with spending more time meeting and getting to know people outside of work. To her, this new life felt more balanced and she appreciated her sense of continued growth and change. She felt less anxious about getting older and more confident about continuing to assess, revise, and plan her later life as she herself wanted it to be.

"Anticipatory socialization" and "concurrent socialization" are fancy terms meaning how you feel about and adjust to a given social role before (anticipatory) and after (concurrent) you actually find yourself in that role. Our society gives unclear and sometimes conflicting messages about exactly how it is that a person is "supposed" to go about getting old or retired. Witness the stereotypes: (1) "All retirees live in Florida or other perpetually sunny places, own poodles with painted toenails, and play golf or fish every day." (2) "All retirees are tired, lonely, depressed, senile, or living in an institution."

Obviously contradictory, right? Such is the nature of stereotypes—never long on rightness or consistency. The point is that if you believe them yourself, you are more apt to be imprisoned by them. On the other hand, if you have accurate information and a healthy respect for yourself and your own abilities, you can worry less about retirement and old age before you arrive at these milestones in your life. You, like Ms. Nelson, can feel better about these roles both before and after you find yourself in them. Knowing what to expect decreases anxiety and increases motivation to plan for retirement and later life, thus facilitating good adjustment.

Consideration of Options

Have you ever found yourself stuck in a situation you didn't like but couldn't change? A situation without options? I once lived and worked in Seattle, a city built around water and linked by bridges. All too often a car stalls in the middle of a bridge and traffic backs up for miles. You can't turn right or left without getting very wet. You can't back up. You can't go forward. You know the feeling. You're stuck. You have no options.

The point is that later life can feel like that if you don't plan for it. If options are prematurely closed to you on the basis of age alone, whether by the rules of society or by your own lack of information and action, you may passively accept a role that is not satisfying to you.

Mrs. Burns, on the other hand, is very much in control of her options. She worked as a homemaker for most of her life. Her husband died many years ago, and now she lives on a meager Social Security check. Her children provide a little money now and then, and they frequently try to persuade Mrs. Burns to leave the low-income housing where she lives and move in with them. She has always cheerfully declined, saying she relishes her privacy and is certain they feel the same way. Even though she has moderately severe arthritis, she plans each day around her household chores, her visits with the "old folks" (Mrs. Burns is eighty-two), and her walk to a downtown department store for morning coffee. Her budget is tight but she plans it to the last cent, and each year buys herself a season ticket to the opera. She speaks and carries herself with an inner conviction and elegance that are enviable at any age.

Mrs. Burns considers her options, sets her priorities, and plans her life in accordance with both. She is changing and growing in later life just as she always has done—with grace, humor, fortitude, and a clear sense of what she wants from life. She accepts nothing passively. She plans ahead.

If you drive across Seattle's bridges enough, you learn to listen to the radio traffic reports and take a different route when there's a problem. You leave earlier. You put books in your car to read if you get stuck. You get used to sometimes being late. In the same way, by planning ahead and thinking of your options clearly, you can make a better life for yourself, regardless of your external circumstances.

Anticipation of Problems

One of the reasons people can adjust to bridge traffic in Seattle is that almost everyone *expects* delay. You can anticipate potential problems with later-life finances, activity, health, or family in plenty of time to find ways of coping effectively.

Consider Robert Parson, an accountant who had planned to continue working to the end of his years. He was part owner in a small firm, and he enjoyed his work and his friends there. He had made few plans for what he would do in the event of retirement. But his wife got cancer, and the two of them decided that before she died they wanted to take an extended trip together. So Mr. Parson sold his share in the business, his wife received what treatment could be given for her illness, and the two of them went to Europe for their dream trip. Mrs. Parson died a year later, and Mr. Parson never regretted their decision to spend those last months together. But now he finds himself without enough capital to reinvest in his company, and he is not really sure what he wants to do with his time. He needs an income but finds employers reluctant to hire a man of his age, in spite of his experience.

Half of all people who will retire within a year do not know what their retirement income will be. Some people expect to be sick or disabled when they reach a certain age. Spouses often find that their relationship is different after one or both partners retire. Many people are surprised to find that they need to think about how they spend their time if they retire. After all, before you retire it certainly *seems* as if there are enough chores and projects to keep you busy for at least twenty years. But as one sixty-seven-year-old retired forestry worker put it, "You can only cut the yard so many times in a week. . . ."

The point is that if you anticipate some of the common financial, health, time, and family problems in later life, you can plan for them. If you don't plan for them, you may find it harder to solve or adjust to them. Perhaps if he had thought it through, Mr. Parson could have made arrangements to take a leave of absence from his work or to return at a later date. Give some thought to how you would deal with potential problems in later life. You can cope better with almost anything if you have planned for it.

Greater Sense of Control—
Better Self-Worth

The improved sense of control that comes from planning is related to the fact that preparation allows you to continue to feel that you have options. You can choose one course of action over others with impunity, given adequate resources and abilities. Feeling powerless is not conducive to mental health, and active planning is an antidote for feelings of helplessness. Therefore, you need to plan your later life, even if you don't want to retire. Things may change, and you want to be ready if and when they do.

Early Monroe's engineering firm had a mandatory retirement policy for the position he held. He did not like to think about retiring because he said it made him feel old. After a couple of years of mentally avoiding the subject, one of his friends retired and Mr. Monroe was galvanized into action by the way this man seemed to drift through his days without purpose. He began to talk seriously with his employers about taking a new position in the company—in a division that did not have a mandatory retirement rule. He was able to arrange a transfer into a challenging new area by taking charge of the situation and actively pursuing his goal.

Believing in yourself as a valuable and worthwhile person is related to feeling capable and prepared in the face of changing roles and expectations. Just having correct information will help you avoid the trap of believing, and therefore acting on, negative stereotypes about retiring and aging. Feeling good about yourself also involves knowing that your life is important and worth savoring for as long as you have it. That means having the courage to plan and the flexibility to take some things as they come.

Another story illustrates: In the winter of 1985 an unusual snowstorm in Seattle brought the hilly city to a near standstill, except for a few stalwart souls on cross-country skis. A beautiful woman in her seventies entered a downtown department store, cheerfully stomping the snow from her shiny red boots. The glow of those boots was matched only by the glow of her cheeks, framed by a mass of flyaway gray curls. Smiling in spite of herself, one of the clerks asked the woman what on earth she was doing out in such weather. "Playing in it," came the instant reply. "Life is what happens to you when you meant to do something else, you know. . . ."

More Positive Attitude—
Decreased Belief in Stereotypes

Dr. W. E. Oaks, a dentist in his late sixties, had begun to decrease the number of patients in his busy practice. He did this more from a sense that it was about time he retired than from any particular desire to do other things. But, as he decreased his practice, he became restless and irritable at home, and his family remarked on the change. He tried to talk about his feelings with his best friend but could not articulate what was wrong. He went to his family doctor, who found no physical problems and referred him to a psychiatrist. In treatment, Dr. Oaks gradually came to realize that his anxiety was related to his recent feeling that his life was nearly over. This idea had come to him when he started decreasing his workload. He discovered that he thought of "old," "retired," "useless," and "finished" as basically synonymous terms. He equated retirement with death and physical illness, in spite of his own good health.

Dr. Oaks had retirement and aging mixed up, and he believed a lot of negative stereotypes about both. He had begun to cut back his practice because of the preconceived idea that a person in his middle sixties should retire. He did not really consider what this might mean to him emotionally or intellectually. What he needed was accurate information and concrete planning to decide whether or not he really wanted to retire at all. When he got the information and worked through some of his anxiety about getting older, he planned a later life that satisfied *him*, not based on some mythical notion of what he "should" do and be as an older person.

Specific Actions

People who plan take specific steps to ensure greater satisfaction for themselves in terms of money, health, relationships, and activity. That people who plan have more money and are more satisfied with their activities, emotional well-being, and physical health may be related to this fact. Making changes that will have significant impact on the quality of your life takes time, self-assessment, knowledge, and action. Making these changes is the goal of your work in this book.

Have you wondered what a "satisfactory" later life really is? The question is appropriate, and it has often been asked by those who criticize the research for being too subjective. Basically, a satisfactory later life is a later life that satisfies you. While this answer may not be specific enough for a scientific study, it serves nicely for our purposes here. You are making this plan for *you*. It is "satisfactory" when you are satisfied.

In summary, planning is consistently the most important predictor of satisfactory adjustment to retirement and later life. As with all things human, the situation is tremendously complex, and involves literally hundreds of difficult-to-control variables. Further, we are only now beginning to study later life, and the truth is, we don't know much about it. We are looking for simple solutions to complicated problems with insufficient information. Let's be pragmatic: (1) It is reasonable to infer, from the information we have, that preparation is a positive factor in adjustment to retirement and later life. (2) There are no negative effects from such preparation. (3) Therefore, making a plan is the best and most accessible way for you to influence your satisfaction in later life in a positive way. In other words, it can't hurt. It *can* help.

Notes

1. C. Taylor, "Developmental conceptions and the retirement process," in *Retirement,* ed. F. M. Carp (New York: Behavioral Publications, Inc., 1972).

2. T. Broderick and B. Glazer, "Leisure participation and the retirement process," *American Journal of Occupational Therapy* 37(1) (1983): 15–22. C. Hendrick, K. S. Wells, and M. V. Faletti, "Social and emotional effects of geographical relocation on elderly retirees," *Journal of Personality and Social Psychology* 42(5) (1982): 951–62. D. C. Charles, "Effect of participation in a pre-retirement program," *Gerontologist* 11(1) (1971): 24–28. R. P. Johnson, "Assessing retirement maturity: Measurement and evaluation," *Guidance* 15(3) (1982): 221–27. I. H. Simpson, K. W. Back, and J. C. McKinney, "Exposure to information on, preparation for, and self-evaluation in retirement," in *Social Aspects of Aging,* eds. I. H. Simpson and J. C. McKinney (Durham, N.C.: Duke University Press, 1966).

3. R. C. Atchley, *The Social Forces in Later Life: An Introduction to Social Gerontology,* (Belmont, Calif.: Wadsworth, 1972).

2 Retirement in America: Transition to Later Life

People have always aged but only recently have they retired.
                                                    —*R. M. Belbin*

What is retirement? Think about it. What does the word bring to mind? Do you see an old guy in a fishing hat? a condo in Florida? poverty? comfortable leisure? relief? boredom? aging? fulfillment? If for you the word conjures up more negative images than positive, you are not alone, regardless of your age. By the dictionary, to retire is to "move away from, to remove oneself from action, to retreat or recede." Look at the definitions. You can see how negative images of retirement arise. Add the general work-oriented and youth ideals of American society today, and you have the most fertile of soil for prejudice and stereotypes.

Now consider aging. What does it mean to get older, to be an older person in our society today? Does it mean you are sick? senile? boring? useless? dying? For all too many people, old and young, this is the image of age. Are these negative images justified? How will they affect you?

How Do Retirement and Aging Fit Together?

Retirement and aging are different but related. To retire is to leave the work you have done for most of your life. To age is to grow older, to keep living. In American society, the event of retirement has become a way of signaling the start of older adulthood. Just think of all the various ways we have of labeling people who have passed this time of life: senior citizen, golden-ager, etc. All of these terms have come to be used almost synonymously with *retiree,* despite the obvious reality that one can get to be older without retiring, or retire without getting older.

Conception, for example, delineates the start of the prenatal period, and birth the start of infancy. Infancy and the various phases of childhood can be separated on the basis of such readily observable events as speaking the first word, taking the first step, or starting school. Adolescence begins around the time of puberty. The events that mark the different phases of the early human life cycle are generally biologically derived and occur at about the same age for most people. After puberty, however, the mile markers become more dependent on the individual. Young adulthood means leaving the nest, right? Does that mean that the thirteen-year-old runaway is an adult, or that the graduate student in his thirties who still lives at home and gets financial assistance is a child? When does middle age start? In the 1960s, middle-aged was anyone over thirty!

Because adult life stage changes depend more on social and individual circumstances than on biology, they don't occur at the same age for everyone. That's why the clearly definable moment of retirement has become a kind of doorway into later life.

Medical advances and better living conditions have increased the human life span dramatically. At first, the consequence was that one could suffer longer from a lot of chronic but not lethal diseases. More recently, however, absolute number of years lived has been leveling off, and advancement has been directed toward increasing the number of healthy years. This is important because one of the problems with being old in America is that, after a certain age and often mysteriously coincident with the age of retirement, one is perceived as a person who is more or less waiting around to die. Sobering, isn't it? To consider that a perfectly alive and capable person is perceived, or worse yet perceives himself or herself, as being about to die for some fifteen to thirty years—what an incredible waste of human resource!

The facts are: All old people are not retired. All retired people are not old. Neither retirement nor aging is invariably associated with sickness, senility, or worthlessness. You retire from a job, not from the rest of your life.

There are as many ways to work and not to work as there are people to devise them. By thinking of later life as continuous with earlier stages, you can more easily view it as important and worthy of your efforts to get the most from it. You will be less likely to get discouraged by stereotypes that are degrading and untrue. You will want to learn about it and prepare for it. You will respect yourself and command the respect of others.

How Did Retirement Develop?

Retirement is a social invention that did not exist in preliterate societies, early in human history. The food supply was based on hunting and gathering, and each person had to bring home enough meat or berries to eat. Anyone who could no longer do so could no longer stay with the tribe, lest all perish. Life was harsh, and survival meant work. Knowledge and experience were of relatively low priority. To stop work was to die.

Thousands of years later, cultures came to be based on agriculture. People stayed in one place and began to own and work the land. The work became more complex, and division of labor was both possible and useful. Knowledge and experience with crops and weather were valued. An older person in this society might no longer be able to plow or harvest the fields, but he or she could teach the farming skills of a lifetime: how to build the best barn, or tend a sick horse, or divert the creek to the south pasture in times of drought. Furthermore, this old person probably owned the land! The "elders" in an agricultural society are important repositories of knowledge about the culture. Retirement remains a foreign concept.

Before World War I, the United States was still basically an agricultural society. After World War I, people began to move to the cities, and the shift to a predominantly urban society began. Work became a job done for someone else, increasingly removed from the final product. The young worker with new skills was more valuable than the old one with experience. The economy was based on factories—making things, and making them faster and better. Few companies had retirement plans, and people (mostly men) simply worked until they could no longer do so, then lived on savings for the relatively short time remaining to them. Social Security did not yet exist.

The Great Depression of the 1930s resulted in massive unemployment and widespread financial hardship. The Social Security Act of 1935 was devised in an attempt to provide some form of income "insurance," to reduce unemployment, and to provide a pension after retirement. Following World War II, private companies and employers began to offer pensions and retirement benefits, following the government model. Today these benefits are an expected part of the package in almost all jobs with larger companies or organizations.

Retirement is a relatively new phenomenon and became nearly universal very rapidly. In 1900, 68 percent of all men over sixty-five years old were still in the labor force. By 1950, the figure was 50 percent, and by 1984, 16.3 percent![1] Why such a rapid shift?

The term "work ethic" has been used in many ways, but it basically refers to the idea that work has a moral and social meaning beyond simply the provision of money with which to buy the necessities of life. From early in European colonization, America was the land of opportunity. The corollary was that those who worked, profited. Rags-to-riches Horatio Alger stories emphasized ambition, honesty, determination, and hard work. Work, in and of itself, took on meaning as the only proper way to spend one's days. It developed an importance beyond simply survival. Work began to be considered a part of one's character. Those who did not work in the marketplace (women, for example) were devalued. At its most dogmatic, the work ethic implies that only someone who is employed in the marketplace is morally and socially worthwhile.

What happened after World War II to promote acceptance of retirement? First was the passage of the Social Security Act, after which the private sector began to provide retirement plans and benefits, making retirement financially feasible for millions. Second, the American economy gradually became more oriented toward performing services rather than producing goods. Technology began to be based on theoretical, rather than applied, knowledge. Knowledge and experience were again valued, with division of labor and decreased need for physical strength to do the work. There was continued economic growth.[2]

A third factor was the growing power of the unions and their leaders, who saw retirement as a way to ensure jobs for younger workers. As the individual worker became further and further removed from the final product of his or her labor, attitudes began to change toward work and the workplace. The belief that work is appropriately the primary focus of activity and source of personal satisfaction began to be questioned. Since the 1940s there has been increasing support for seeking personal gratification in pursuits outside of the job market. In short, the power of the work ethic has declined and appears to be continuing to do so. The concept of retirement has continuously gained acceptance.

Retirement is here to stay in our society, at least in the foreseeable future. But you must remember that there is nothing biologically or spiritually ordained about it. Retirement developed out of cultural and historical fabric. It was a solution to certain social problems. Retirement may or may not be appropriate for you.

Why Sixty-five?

Why do we retire at sixty-five? Perhaps on the basis of scientific evidence that this is biologically or psychologically the best time to replace older workers? Or because productivity is much lower after this age? None of the above. The concept of compulsory retirement and the use of age sixty-five as the retirement age originated with Chancellor Bismarck of Germany in the middle 1800s. The average life expectancy at the time was forty-five years. The government's coffers were therefore fairly unlikely to be emptied by people who were forced to retire. The choice of age sixty-five as "the age to retire" is entirely arbitrary.

How Does All This Affect You?

Retirement is relatively new. In the social stock market, the work ethic has plummeted, replaced by the more common attitude that work is something you do to get money to do what you really want to do. As one cynic put it, "Work is what you do now so you don't have to do it later." Nowadays, in fact, the person who chooses not to retire may be viewed as unusual, if not downright selfish and socially irresponsible.

This is tricky ground on which to be looking for a culturally acceptable and personally satisfactory way to spend your later life. Like a city that grows too fast to be adequately planned, and thus has bizarre street arrangements and insufficient parking, the social institution of retirement sprang onto the scene and became almost universal so fast that society has not developed an internally consistent system. You, therefore, get a lot of confusing messages. First you may be required to retire, then be told that you aren't worth much unless you're working. Or you may get the idea that retirement is good and find out only after the fact that as a retired person you must live in poverty or fit some stereotype that has little to do with you as an individual.

For most of you, retirement is an option and living into old age is a given. In our society, entry into later life is marked most conveniently by the event of retirement. If you are old, retired or retiring, you are still alive. Big news, right? Better yet, if you are old, retired, or retiring, you are still a contributing member of society. We use retirement and work to define ourselves and our lives in certain ways. That does not mean that we must allow either to imprison us in unfulfilling lives (at any age).

Retirement should be a choice and should not be forced solely on the basis of chronological age. The key element is change and transition, not loss and decline. In fact, change—adaptation to the new and leaving behind what came before—is the essence of life. (Remember the seventy-year-old in her red boots "playing in the snow.") The infant leaves the safety of the womb to start life in a new world. The baby gives up being carried to walk and to independently explore new territory. The child leaves parents for friends and leaves home for school. School gives way to work. The adolescent becomes adult. Adult becomes parent, and parent becomes grandparent. Each of these changes requires adjustment. The basic person remains the same.

To properly integrate aging and retirement, you must not believe the morbid absurdity that people sit around waiting for death for all the years they live after retirement. You can plan for this time and live it meaningfully. You are still yourself, and you can draw on the experience and resources of earlier years.

Perhaps in looking for specific role definitions and social norms or standards for later living, we miss the point entirely. Think of yourself as a flowering tree. In the very beginning, as a seed, you may be measurable only by such things as weight or circumference. As a seedling, you begin to have height and a different shape. Variations and branchings continue to be added as you grow. At maturity, characteristics such as shape and form, color and leaves, flowers and branches become more important than simple numerical measurements.

Failure to recognize and credit the later years as an integral part of the life cycle is a problem because it promotes a kind of social, intellectual, and emotional amputation of the life of a human being in full flower. The trunk is sturdy and strong. Its roots and branches extend in all directions. It cannot be measured accurately just by weight or height or age. In the same way, the tasks, rewards, and challenges of this fully differentiated human being cannot reasonably be expected to be identical to those of the infant, the adolescent, or the young adult.

Retirement is just one part of the tree of your life, and its meaning will vary with different individual circumstances. At this branch point, *you* are taking time to reassess and possibly change how you spend your time. You may stop the work you did in the earlier part of your life. You may continue but spend fewer hours at it. You may change occupations entirely. You may decide to make no changes at all. The careful consideration of options, the time of reassessment is what's important. Later life is yours, and it encompasses all of what makes you a unique and valuable person.

How you use this time in your life is your choice. To make changes, you will set goals for yourself that promote individual satisfaction with both your work status and the rest of your life. You will maintain your place in society by learning to deal with whatever prejudice the culture dishes out. You will maintain your self-esteem.

Planning for later life, with its attendant decisions and implementation of active steps to improve your life, will help. The goal is to integrate the many areas of your life into a satisfactory whole, the nature and quality of which is determined by your own unique characteristics. You are far less likely to retire from *life* if you can see the later years as part of a whole—a continuum from birth to death in which each phase has rhythm and a beauty of its own.

Notes

1. G. Collins, "As more men retire early, more women work longer," *The New York Times* (April 3, 1986). United States Bureau of Labor Statistics, 1984.

2. F. C. Pampel, *Social Change and the Aged: Recent Trends in the United States* (New York: Free Press, 1981).

3 Retirement and You: What to Expect

Absence of occupation is not rest, a mind quite vacant is a mind distressed.

—William Cowper (1713–1800)

Think about how many times you have seen or heard the phrase "retiree" used generically to refer to an older person—as if it tells you anything at all about the person in question. Retirement means different things to different people. It can be used to force people out of jobs by means of mandatory retirement rules, forced early retirement, job discrimination, or reassignment to boring or otherwise undesirable work. There may be subtle peer pressure to discourage continued work, as well as financial disincentives provided by the Social Security system. When unwanted, retirement may seem like a punishment for having reached a certain age.

On the other hand, retirement may be a socially graceful way of escaping a job that has become difficult, boring, or unfulfilling for some reason. It may be seen as a reward for years of service, making way for a new generation of workers.

Retirement means different things to different people mainly because *work* means different things to different people. Consider Arthur Conn. He has had his job as a chemist in a laboratory for more than twenty years. And that's exactly what he considers it—a job; something he does to make money for himself and his family. He does his job faithfully and well. But his real "life work"—what makes him feel alive—is music. He plays pedal steel guitar in a country band three nights a week. His basement at home is his practice studio, and he dreams of retirement—he can't wait—as a chance to pursue his musical interest full time. His nickname in the lab is the "cowboy chemist."

Martin Lifton is also a chemist, in a laboratory across town. His

18

work there *is* his life, and he spends much of his free time at his lab bench, on his own, working on a procedure to improve the durability of exterior house paint. He is respected by his coworkers for his up-to-date knowledge and his meticulous attention to detail. He does not like to think of retirement at all. His fellow workers call him "Beaker."

Do you see the difference between these two men? For Arthur Conn, being a chemist is simply a job. For Dr. Lifton, the same work is an integral part of himself, with importance far beyond the provision of a paycheck. Dr. Conn looks forward to retirement as an exciting opportunity. He is personally much more involved in his music than in his weekday occupation. Martin Lifton has invested himself in the laboratory. To retire from work would be to leave a part of himself behind.

Neither of these attitudes is right or wrong, but the implications are different. Conn already knows that he will retire, and his plans center around how to maintain his financial and physical health and persuade his wife to go on the road with the band! Lifton needs to think about whether to retire at all. There is no mandatory rule about it at his lab, but he will be the first to stay on past age sixty-five. He also has to consider how he can still work on his projects if he later decides to retire.

Is Retirement Harmful?

The meaning and importance of work and retirement vary with individual values and circumstances. To make informed decisions about retirement, you should know how it usually affects people. Is it harmful? What changes can you expect in terms of health, relationships, and money?

True or false: A significant number of people waste away physically or mentally once they retire. You are already ahead of the class if you answered false. People who retire do not die or develop medical or psychological problems more often than those who do not.[1] Still, these ideas have been remarkably persistent, testimony perhaps to the tenacity (rather than veracity) of the negative stereotypes of old people in America.

Retirement itself is not intrinsically bad. In one group of retired people, 75 percent said that retirement was mostly good, over 75 percent rated their own health as good or excellent, and more than 90 percent said that they were mostly satisfied with their lives.[2] For some people, what is most harmful is their own belief that their lives are over once they retire. They do not plan, they are needlessly anxious, and they miss out on what could be a rewarding time of life.

Retirement and Physical Health

Most of you will retire. Many newspaper reporters delight in stories about old Mr. So-and-So who smilingly accepts his gold watch at his retirement party, then drops dead of a heart attack on the subway home.

You must believe that *retirement won't kill you or make you sick*. Before retirement became a social institution, the relationship between physical health and retirement was clear. Only debilitating sickness or an accident resulted in a person who did not work for a living. If you became ill you stopped working, you "withdrew from action," you retired. If you remained healthy and sound, you worked.

Now, somewhat ironically, healthy older Americans are retiring earlier and earlier. Debilitation and stopping work are no longer always connected. Our society is in the process of uncoupling physical health from retirement, a situation that allows you many more options once you understand and can take advantage of this opportunity. You can retire from teaching and open a bakery or earn a degree in cultural anthropology. You can sell your dry cleaning business and travel in your motor home. You can stop being a homemaker and become an auto mechanic. (Please note that I did not say that these things would be easy, only that you have options!)

How do you know that retirement won't kill you or make you sick? The health of people who continue to work is being scientifically compared with those who have retired. So far, no significant difference has been found in self-reported health status, frequency of physical symptoms, blood pressure, cholesterol levels, or ratings of physical health based on medical examinations.[3]

Subjective reports are also interesting. In a study of people ages sixty-five through seventy, the proportion described as being in moderately good health was the same in both retired and nonretired groups. When decline in physical health was present, the older people themselves did not attribute the change to retirement.[4] In spite of the fact that about 50 percent of people cite decline in health as a *reason* for retirement, fewer than 5 percent of people who have retired report decreased health after retirement, and 25–40 percent report improvement.[5]

What do all these numbers mean? Basically, no matter how these different studies sort out the different percentages, there is no objective evidence to support the idea that retirement is hazardous to your health, and individual older people themselves do not perceive it to be so. Retirement, physical health, and quality of later life are certainly intertwined for you in many ways, but you need not expect that simply choosing to retire will either kill you or make you sick.

It is important, however, to consider how work and health are related for you. If you are a surgeon with moderately severe arthritis, the effect on your continued work is apt to be very different than the same degree of arthritis in a corporate executive, for example. Certainly the state of your physical health may influence your decisions about retirement. You can avoid the sense of helplessness which sometimes attends changes made for health reasons by planning ahead. Vincent Bretti suffered a serious heart attack at age sixty-one. While he convalesced at home, he decided that if he had another heart attack he would close his plumbing business and remain available to the new owners for occasional contract work. By planning ahead, he avoided the dread of such an event and was able to be humorously philosophical about it. "Planning makes me feel better," Bretti said. "If the next one kills me, I won't need to work anyway! And if it doesn't, I can look forward to something new."

Retirement and Mental Health

Retirement does not cause mental illness. That's right. Retirement not only won't kill you or make you sick, it also will not make you crazy or senile or even unhappy! There are certainly people for whom retirement is an unmitigated mental disaster. But being able to adjust is the norm.[6] The exceptions prove the rule, but they also contribute to the same old myth: *Some* people who are old do poorly if they retire; therefore *all* old people do poorly if they retire. This is not true, but sometimes if you expect a problem, you will find one.

How does retirement affect mental health? The answer for you depends on how many other things you have to cope with at the same time, your general sense of well-being, your physical health, and your previous ability to cope with change. A fundamental point is that the emotional needs met for you at work will still need to be met if you retire. If you don't get much out of the work you do, you are not likely to miss it much if you retire. On the other hand, if work is your only source of social contact or your main source of self-esteem, then you need other ways to meet these needs if you retire.

Tex Badden worked for twenty-seven years as a private driver for a number of wealthy executives in Sacramento. When he was fifty-eight years old, he suffered a mild stroke which left him with almost imperceptible weakness on one side. But, as a consequence of the stroke, he developed seizures that left him unable to continue driving. Being unable to drive—he'd never really done anything else—made him feel lonely and depressed, without friends or things to do, and he thought long and often about suicide. Was retirement to blame for Mr. Badden's unhappiness? He had seemed happy and friendly before. He was intelligent and well liked by his clients, and he lived well. What happened to him? As he talked, it became apparent that his job had indeed suited him. He had worked fairly long hours and his only "social life" was talking to his clients as he drove. As a result, he knew a great deal about them, but no one was really close to him. He was proud of his association with these upper-crust people and derived a lot of his self-esteem from the fact that they regarded him highly. He had also made good money but had made no plans for retirement. You can see the problem. Mr. Badden's life before retirement had little balance. It was built almost entirely around his work, and it collapsed when he retired.

At the other extreme is Barney Cole, who drove a taxi for twenty years in San Francisco. Mr. Cole did not particularly like driving a taxi (and would tell this to anyone in earshot, especially passengers), but it paid the bills and gave him enough flexibility to pursue his avid interest in gardening. At the age of sixty-two, Mr. Cole also had a mild stroke and was forced to retire somewhat before he had planned. That same year he lost his son in an auto accident. For about six months, Mr. Cole and his wife mourned the loss of their child. They had little interest in their gardens, and Mr. Cole spent hours in his favorite chair vacantly gazing out the window. Slowly but surely, though, he began to adjust. Neighbors came to ask his advice on their spring planting, as they had for years. He tramped into the woods behind his house to find favorite cuttings for each. He planted flowers and fruit. He gave advice and assistance. He began to live again. At the end of the second year of his physically forced retirement, Mr. Cole and his wife opened a small plant nursery—his lifelong dream.

Both of these men were obliged to retire somewhat before the usual age because of medical conditions that interfered with their work but did not debilitate them a great deal in other ways. Neither had made very secure financial plans, though Mr. Cole did have some savings. Why was Barney Cole able to adjust when Tex Badden was not? Such a question is never easy to answer, but certainly an important factor was that Mr. Cole's emotional investment in his work was much lower than that of Mr. Badden. He met most of his emotional needs outside of his work—with family and friends as well as through absorbing and satisfying work in his garden. That doesn't mean that it is bad to be invested in your work in a meaningful way, only that if work is your sole source of emotional well-being, you must make a solid plan for how to get that emotional well-being in other ways if you retire.

Retirement may thus "unmask" a mental health problem that was obscured by the activity and structure of work in earlier years. In Mr. Badden's case, that problem had to do with his difficulty making relationships with other people except very superficially. Because any change requires adjustment, retirement can be the "last straw" in a series of events that lead to difficulty. Perhaps, for example, Mr. Badden could have coped with retirement better if he had saved a bit more money or if he had not suffered the stroke. On the other hand, Mr. Cole's resources for coping could have been overwhelmed if his wife had died that year. Any failure of adjustment will show itself in altered mental health.

Consider a different situation. Suppose you are one of the 5–10 percent of people who develop mild, stable memory loss in later life. Further suppose that you are a telephone operator and have to remember strings of numbers to be able to do your job effectively. After two or three years of struggling to remember the numbers as you once did, you are anxious and easily upset. You are not enjoying your job anymore. What do you think will happen to your self-esteem after retirement? You'll probably feel a lot better!

Mental health and retirement, then, are connected in a way that is not determined by the characteristics of retirement as an event, but rather by its meaning within the context of your life. What is your life like outside of work? What needs are met for you at work? What other things are happening to you at the same time? How well have you coped with changes in the past? What is the status of your physical health, your finances, your relationships? How do you feel about getting older? All of these factors affect your emotional adjustment to retirement.

Trouble adjusting emotionally to retirement is to be expected if circumstances and resources do not allow you to meet your physical, psychological, and social needs in the usual way. If such a *mismatch* develops, you will need to recognize it for what it is and deal with it accordingly. Prevention is better, however. Think about what you get out of going to work. The value of your paycheck, for example, is not to be underestimated. For some people, getting that paycheck is not only a financial but also a psychological necessity. That is, the money is a symbol of independence and accomplishment. It says to the world and to the individual: "I lay this carpet or sell this product well enough to get paid for it." If this is an important source of satisfaction for you, then volunteer work is not going to meet that need after retirement. You'll need a paying job.

Mental or physical challenge is another emotional need that may be met at work. The axiom "Use it or lose it" applies to brains and bodies in all kinds of ways. If you don't exercise your muscles regularly, they get weak and out of shape. The same holds true for using your mind. You need regular mental activity that is challenging and invigorating. Work may provide that for you. If you retire, you will have to meet that need in other ways. Options include taking classes, organizing a special-interest group, going into business for yourself, volunteering, teaching—whatever gives you enough of a challenge to keep you in good mental shape.

Work may help you feel productive and useful. Many people in the "helping professions," for example, gain personal satisfaction from being able to help others. Nurses, social workers, teachers, and doctors are obvious examples, but many other people feel defined by their work in some way.

Feeling useful and productive is important in maintaining self-esteem and also is part of the larger picture of our work-oriented society. Think, for example, about parties you've attended where the guests did not know each other well. Someone asks what you do. If you answer with your occupation, more questions follow, and a conversation ensues during which you and the other person get to know each other better. If you say you are retired, there may be a polite "Oh, that's nice" and a rather quick end to the conversation unless you can "rescue" it by bringing up other topics. In fact, many retired people learn to answer with their former occupations to avoid this problem. You are obviously the same interesting person you always were, and you need to feel valued and worthwhile. That feeling may come from your work more than you realize.

Finally, people are often surprised by how much their social contacts narrow if they retire. Regular daily contact with other people is a frequently unrecognized emotional need that is met at work. People do differ in terms of how much they like to be around other people, but human beings are basically herd animals and it is a rare person indeed who has no need of others—even if only to argue with them! If you retire, the number of people you see every day will probably drastically decrease. Like many of the changes that come with retirement, this may seem all right and even desirable at first. But the reality is that most people choose what they do for a living the same way they choose hobbies, spouses, or friends, because that choice meets certain emotional needs or desires. So even if, as manager of your own store, you spend the better part of each day wishing that this person or that problem would get out of your life, you had best think about what you will do to replace them when you retire. Don't just assume you'll be glad to be rid of the whole mess. You may be surprised to find that you miss that mess later on.

Retirement and Relationships

Retirement is change, and change requires adjustment—both for you and for all those in any relationships in which you are involved. The relationship may be with a marital partner, friends, children, or other family members. To whatever extent retirement affects you, it will affect the people who are close to you. How does retirement affect relationships?

Marriage

For a married couple, deciding whether or not to retire means deciding who will retire, when, and to do what? Many older women working today entered the work force later than their spouses and may not be ready to retire when their husbands are. As noted in a previous chapter, about 50 percent of men over age sixty-five were working in 1950. By 1984 only 16.3 percent were working. By contrast, in 1950 about 10 percent of women over age sixty-five worked outside the home, declining only to 7.5 percent by 1984. Also, more and more women between the ages of fifty-five and sixty-four are working—27 percent in 1950 and 41.7 percent in 1984.[7] These numbers mean that you may have a conflict of interests to resolve if one of you wants to retire as soon as possible and the other isn't ready to think about it at all. You must be considerate of each other's goals and feelings. While men often say that their wives support their decision to retire, many women report being pressured to retire.

There is no evidence to support the notion that loss of the work role has less impact on women than on men. When you think about it, such a proposition also does not make sense. If work is important to you, then retirement has meaning and requires adjustment, whether you're a man or a woman.

If you and your spouse both work outside the home, you will need to talk openly about whether or not you both want to retire and, if so, when and to what degree—partially or fully. Some women who entered the work force later because they were caring for children in their earlier years want to keep working after their husbands retire. Others take early retirement options so that the couple can retire together. No one way is inherently right or wrong unless you have trouble negotiating your wishes with those of the person you're living with. You need to consider the pros and cons of each option and make the decision together.

For example, you may assume that once your partner retires, the two of you will spend more time together and communicate better simply for that reason. The truth of the matter is that the relationship is apt to continue pretty much as it is. Conflicts may arise because you are together more or because you have different expectations of each other or the relationship in later life. You will not automatically communicate better just because you are in the same house more. On the positive side, however, the mere fact of retirement will not damage the relationship. The changes that come with retirement are specific. You can plan, and you can adjust.

The same holds true if one of you has worked inside the home and the other outside. Having both spouses at home can change things drastically: "Now that Fred's retired, I have half as much money and twice as much husband." For a woman who chose the traditional role of homemaker, having her partner around the house much more after he retires can change her accustomed pattern of activity. In addition, he may want to help with things she'd rather do herself (especially if his own activities are not well planned). Conflicts over "turf" are fairly common, but you can negotiate new arrangements for sharing space and duties before the conflicts get out of hand.[8]

Other potential problem areas include how you spend your money, how much time you spend together and apart, what you do with your time, and how close you are to other family and friends. You have to think and talk about how each of these will affect the relationship. Now is better than later, for example, to find out that your spouse and that work chum you secretly despise are talking about buying a recreational vehicle together and driving to Alaska to fish!

Children

Your children may have their own expectations about what things will be like if you retire. They may expect (hope) you'll stay with their kids a lot. They may be worried about how much financial or other support they will need to provide for you. They may expect you to continue to support them. You may have expectations of your children: to live with them at some point or never at all, to spend more (or less) time with grandchildren. The point is that people often have different ideas and silent assumptions about things. Opening lines of communication on delicate matters before they become active problems will save misunderstandings, hurt feelings, and conflicts later. Just as people are unique, so are families. Styles of interacting and patterns of support vary widely. You will need plenty of time to talk about your plans with the important people in your life.

Grandchildren

Nowadays, people who work and have children and families know that grandparents sometimes provide much needed continuity and stability in broken lives and broken families. This kind of grandparental role may not be for everyone, but it can be rewarding for some.

Friends

Think about your general style with regard to other people. Do you like having a lot of people around you or do you prefer to be alone more often than not? The number of unrelated people you see daily is likely to be sharply reduced after retirement, at least initially. What will that mean for you? If you like and want to be around many different people each day, plan your later-life activity to take that into account.

Society

You have a relationship with yourself, your family, and your friends that is largely based on the person you know yourself to be. That person goes to work, makes a home, cares for others, laughs, cries, thinks, talks, cooks hamburgers, and walks in the park. You also have a relationship with society as a whole. Unfortunately, however, that relationship is not based so much on your personal traits and qualities as on certain demographic facts. One of those facts is whether or not you work. What will the attitudes of people in particular and society as a whole mean for you? One of my young cousins once referred to her grandmother as "retarded." When questioned, she replied that this meant that "Meemaw hadn't worked in a long time." What is amusing in this context may not be so in others. How would you react?

Relationships are important, and retirement brings about changes that require adjustment, negotiation, and compromise. Retirement changes are entwined with others arising from increased age, and both individuals and the relationships they establish have different levels of flexibility and coping power. Maintaining your relationships after retirement is mostly a matter of managing expectations and assumptions.

Retirement and Money

The average person's income is cut in half upon retirement. Though it's generally true that retirement doesn't have an across-the-board negative impact for most people, money is the exception to that rule. This is why you need to fully understand what your financial picture will be when and if you retire *before* you make any irrevocable decisions. Retirement is a definite risk in terms of your monetary security, and you must plan accordingly. (This is such a crucial aspect of retirement planning that many "how to retire" books concentrate mainly on finances.)

What happens to expenses if you retire? Because of such things as tax benefits, discounts for "seniors," and lower clothing and transportation costs, most people can maintain about the same standard of living after retirement with 70–80 percent of their preretirement income. Remember, however, that how much money you need after retirement depends on what you want to do, and that what you "save" by not working may be offset somewhat by the cost of your new activities, increased property taxes, or increased utility costs because you are at home more. Furthermore, if your income decreases to 50 percent of preretirement level and your expenses only decrease to 80 percent, you have an immediately obvious problem. Your later-life financial plan must close this gap.

Old Age, Survivors, and Disability Insurance (OASDI), commonly known as Social Security, is the basic building block of retirement income for most Americans. As the long name implies, it is technically a social insurance program, with benefits distributed on the basis of past contributions, without regard for current income or assets. The idea is that you get back in retirement what you put in while you worked. For some years however, inflation has outpaced Social Security income so that most people actually get back much more than they put in. This can't continue indefinitely, as a portion of the federal deficit is used to cover the shortfall. Fortunately for you, as you consider your retirement, you can be sure of the continuing concern of lawmakers in trying to solve this problem without reducing Social Security benefits. Older people vote, and politicians grow old and retire as well!

Other sources of retirement income include savings and other income-producing assets (rental property, for example), private pensions, and various forms of government aid, including Supplemental Security Income (SSI), food stamps, Medicaid, and subsidized housing. SSI and other forms of public assistance only go to those whose income and assets are below a certain level.

Of course, even though you're "retired," you still can be earning money from work. However, despite the passage of the 1978 Federal Age Discrimination in Employment Act, only about 10 percent of American men and women continue to work beyond the age of sixty-five.

Why do so few people continue to work in later life? Given the respectable opportunity, some individuals would simply prefer to retire from a job they don't particularly like. However, age discrimination may take subtle forms. There may be social pressure to retire. Or the pressure may come from the employer. More experienced workers are more expensive, and this has stimulated the trend toward early retirement, taken in spite of decreased benefits. Reversal of this trend, along with abolition of mandatory retirement based solely on age, could be part of a solution to the problem of dwindling Social Security reserves. For social good, as well as for the good of the Social Security program, it does not make sense for the government to actively discourage older people from working. Under what is called the retirement earnings test, the Social Security recipient's benefits are cut by one dollar for every two dollars earned over a certain amount. This is essentially a 50 percent tax on earnings, what an economist would label a "disincentive."

Another major deterrent to someone who wants to work in their sixties and seventies is the insidious—and therefore harder to overcome—belief that older people can't, shouldn't, or at least shouldn't want to work. Why mention this again in talking about money and retirement? Because if you believe you can't or shouldn't work in later life, you have closed off a potential source of income. You may not be able to afford that.

Not having enough money puts you at risk for a difficult later life, and retirement puts you at risk for not having enough money. There are no magic numbers for how much money is enough and no uniformly applicable ways to make sure you get that magic amount. As with everything else, what you need and want must be coordinated with what you have and can get.

Notes

1. S. G. Haynes, A. J. McMichael, and H. A. Tyroler, "Survival after early and normal retirement," *Journal of Gerontology* 33 (2) (March 1978): 269–78. D. J. Ekerdt, "Effects of retirement on health," from the VA Normative Aging Study in Boston, *Medical Aspects of Human Sexuality* 18 (3) (March 1984): 85. A. Macbride, "Retirement as a life crisis: myth or reality?", *Canadian Psychiatric Association Journal* 21 (8) (December 1976): 547–56. G. F. Streib, J. Streib, and C. J. Schneider, *Retirement in American Society: Impact and Process* (Ithaca and London: Cornell University Press, 1971).

2. C. Hendrick, K. S. Wells, and M. V. Faletti, "Social and emotional effects of geographical relocation on elderly retirees," *Journal of Personality and Social Psychology* 42 (5) (1982): 951–62.

3. See note 1 above.

4. See note 1 above.

5. G. F. Streib, "Two views of retirement: In the clinic and in the community," in *Clinical Aspects of Aging*, 2d ed., ed. W. Reichel (Baltimore and London: Williams & Wilkins, 1983). C.Eisdorfer, "Adaptation to loss of work," in *Retirement*, ed. F. M. Carp (New York: Behavioral Publications, Inc., 1972). Also see note 1 above.

6. See note 1 above.

7. G. Collins, "As more men retire early, more women work longer," *The New York Times* (April 3, 1986).

8. L. P. Bradford and M. I. Bradford, *Retirement: Coping with Emotional Upheavals* (Chicago: Nelson-Hall, 1979).

4 Aging, Ageism, and Attitude

How old would you be if you didn't know how hold you was?
—*Satchel Paige (a professional baseball pitcher at age fifty-nine)*

Just as retirement has certain meanings and implications in our society, so also does aging. If you are a member of a minority group or a woman, you may already know what it's like to find yourself cast in a stereotypical role that bears little resemblance to how you really are. Retirement generally signals that you've reached at least middle age in a society that tends to categorize you by your years. The goal of this chapter is to give you some accurate information about what you can expect from society as an older person. Use the three A's—aging, ageism, and attitude—to help you remember these three important truths:

1. Aging is a biological process. It is often wrongly confused with such things as retirement, sickness, or uselessness. Aging is getting older. Your body becomes gradually, usually not drastically, less vigorous in certain ways. Your mind is part of your body. It changes in some ways and stays the same in others.

2. Ageism is a prejudice. It is a sociocultural phenomenon founded upon myth. Ageism favors youth over years.

3. Attitude is an individual matter. It refers to the fact that the most harmful stereotype about you is the one you believe yourself. What you think of yourself is a crucial part of what you are.

Aging

Aging is a biological and psychological process that is often confused with a number of other things such as retirement, sickness,

31

senility, death, rolelessness, and uselessness. There is clear and present danger to the quality of your later life if you do not learn the distinctions.

First, remember that aging is a positive thing if you consider the alternative. Second, aging is universal and inevitable as long as you live. Why should you be reminded of these facts? Because you must remember that retirement, sickness, senility, and devaluation are neither universal nor inevitable. You have options and choices as an older person.

Aging means life, and life is what we are about here. To understand and appreciate the difference between aging and ageism is to give yourself the best chance of looking forward to later life as a time of change and growth, of challenge and reward, of fulfillment and satisfaction.

Agnes Elliot is seventy-seven years old. She is on welfare. She lives in subsidized housing. Her medical benefits do not include dental work and her dentures don't fit. She has trouble getting to the grocery store because her arthritis makes bus rides difficult. She eats one meal a day and is constantly weak and shaky. She doesn't feel much like doing anything, and she is lonely. Ms. Elliot is a victim of poverty, not of aging.

Harold Forkes has plenty of money but spends most of it on his hospital bills. At sixty-three, he has had two heart attacks and a mild stroke which left him somewhat weak in his left arm and hand. His feet swell during the day and he is short of breath climbing stairs. He has to stop frequently to rest. Mr. Forkes is ill, not simply aging.

Willy Graves is in good physical health at the age of fifty-nine, a high school track coach, but in the past year he's lost forty pounds and his zest for life. He can't sleep at night and he worries constantly about dying or losing all of his savings. He can't concentrate on his work anymore, he forgets things at times, and he sometimes contemplates suicide. Mr. Graves is depressed, not just aging.

Inez Jankowitz, sixty-eight, has worked behind the counter in the same cafeteria for twenty years. She is physically spry and her mind is clear. She takes fewer "sick days" than the twenty-year-old who has just been hired to replace her because, her boss says, "a person your age should retire and take it easy." She doesn't want to retire or to take it easy. Mrs. Jankowitz is suffering from age prejudice, not aging.

Paul Innes retired from his factory job as a machinist at age sixty-five. Two years later his wife complains that he's driving her crazy being home all the time. He has taken to watching the soap operas all day and the sitcoms at night. Occasionally he goes out for a beer with one of his former buddies from work, but he seems to have little to say to them or to anyone else. This is retirement without adequate planning, not aging.

Rosemarie Fogarty is ninety-two and in a nursing home after a massive stroke left her comatose. For several weeks she has been slowly sinking, and there is an ominous rattle when she breathes. Ms. Fogarty is dying, not aging.

Ernie Klineman is active and alert at seventy-five. Ten years ago he gladly retired from his job as an installer for the telephone company, but for the first year he couldn't seem to figure out what to do with himself. Finally, more out of boredom than anything else, he decided to take a cooking class at the community college. He liked working in a kitchen, so he took a part-time job as a cook. After two years he opened a tiny coffee shop near his old office, which these days is packed every morning and noon with people who love his homemade doughnuts, fresh coffee, and cheerful conversation. Sometimes they have to speak up a little so he can catch their orders and wait an extra minute or two for service when his arthritis is acting up, but nobody seems to mind. Mr. Klineman has recently confided in several of his regular customers that he's thinking about selling his coffee shop because he wants to see Europe "before I get too old . . ." *That* is normal, healthy aging!

Ageism

Ageism is a prejudice. Like other prejudices, it is founded on ignorance and maintained by stereotype. Such stereotypes are self-perpetuating, since they are held by many older people themselves. The big difference between ageism and other forms of prejudice is that we all hope to live long enough to become old. Alexander Comfort observes "White racists don't turn black, male chauvinists don't become women, anti-Semites don't wake up and find themselves Jewish—but we have a lifetime of indoctrination with the idea of difference and inferiority of the old, and on reaching old age we may be prejudiced against ourselves."[1]

In spite of ever-increasing numbers of older people, ours is still a very youth-oriented society. All kinds of otherwise sensible, thoughtful people have misconceptions about the elderly and hold prejudices against the old. Learn the facts to avoid the trap of believing the stereotypes about yourself. If you find yourself not doing something you really want to do, or being denied something you really want, solely on the basis of chronological age, think about age prejudice. The first step in solving any problem is to clearly identify it.

Prejudice, by definition, results in loss of personal freedom for its victims. Such denial of freedom is particularly effective if it can be made to seem like a privilege. Black slaves were supposed to be glad they didn't have to worry about running their own lives. Women were supposed to be glad they didn't have to get out in the mean old world and work for a living. Old people should be glad the law "allows" them to retire at a certain arbitrary age, to enjoy a "life of leisure," as if older people were children with no responsibilities, few roles, and little of value to contribute. Think how often you hear remarks about a "cute" old woman or man and how marvelous it is that they look/move/get along as well as they do. Barring some debilitating illness, why shouldn't they? To measure our surprise in this regard is to measure the extent of our confusion between healthy longevity and the debilitation that sometimes occurs just before death.

Attitudes about what life is like at certain ages may not have kept pace with increasing life expectancy. In the time of the Roman Empire, average life expectancy was twenty-three years. In 1900 in the United States it was forty-seven years. Now, at age sixty-five, the average person can expect to live at least sixteen more years, and at age seventy-five, another ten. While baby mortality may account for some of the low average life expectancies of earlier times, certainly there were not very many people living past the age of sixty-five at the time. People now are often retired from adult financial and role responsibilities some ten to twenty years before they have any serious impairment in function. Old people "have problems in our society because it takes them so long to die these days. Society defines them as person-about-to-die, regardless of biological competences, and, as such, they are held to be without significant social value."[2]

Society will soon have to reckon with its injustices to the old. Today one in seven Americans is over the age of sixty. There are an estimated 36.1 million people in this group—15.6 percent of the population. The projected figure for the year 2050 is 67 million—21.7 percent of the population.[3] That's a lot of voters!

The large number of older people has not dispelled the myths and inaccuracies about getting old. Many people still believe that all old people are sick or senile, depressed or lonely, bored or sexless, mostly in nursing homes and barely able to get around. Some people do have these problems. Most do not. Many who do not have these problems still believe the stereotypes and consider themselves the exception rather than the rule. Remember that the stereotypes of ageism are not the realities of aging. Instead, there is a spectrum of styles across a range of norms during later life just as there is during any other phase of life.

You need weapons to fight ageism. Two important ones are knowledge and the ability to think of yourself as an individual, regardless of your age. There are indeed biological, psychological, and social changes associated with the aging process. But there are also many half truths and untruths about aging that are used to devalue you as an older person. You won't even begin the fight, much less win it, if you harbor within yourself the idea that it is somehow "natural" to be debilitated, isolated, depressed, or just plain unhappy when you are old.

Biological Aspects of Ageism

Remember the following:

1. Age is not synonymous with illness.
2. Old or young, some people get sick and some do not.
3. People who get sick deserve careful evaluation and treatment.
4. Older people can and do benefit from treatment.
5. If cure is not possible, adaptation almost always is.

Comfort tells the story of a 104-year-old man who went to the doctor because his knee was stiff. He was told that at his age he should expect his knee to be stiff. To that the old man replied, "Well, my left knee is 104, too, and it doesn't hurt!"[4]

How does ageism use biological changes to the detriment of the old? Ageism weaves skeins of myth around threads of truth, so that it becomes difficult for people to imagine old age as anything more than a horrible downhill slide. Certain issues are more vulnerable than others to ageist embroidery.

Hearing, intellect, and sexuality strongly affect the older person's (and everyone's) mobility, interpersonal relationships, and sense of self-worth. Perhaps not coincidentally, ageist foolishness surrounds these issues.

First, consider how common it really is to be sick and physically disabled in old age. Acute illness causes more days of restricted activity in older people, but older people are *less* often affected by acute illness than their younger counterparts. Although 86 percent of the elderly have one or more chronic health problems, 95 percent live in the community, and 81 percent do so without outside help.[5]

Regrettably, in our society we *expect* older people to have physical affliction. There are consequences for such expectations. For example, some hearing loss, especially in the upper registers, is common among older people. In one study, 34 percent of deaf older Americans had never had a hearing test.[6] Imagine how appalled we would be if a third of our deaf young people had never had their hearing tested and would not be encouraged to do so because their deafness was considered "natural." You need your senses to maintain appropriate interaction with the environment—to get along sensibly in the world. Hearing loss has been associated with impaired sense of reality, suspiciousness, paranoia, and depression.[7] You deserve to have hearing problems carefully evaluated and managed. Because deafness is relatively common in old age does not mean it is always untreatable.

"Senile" is a word that has been abused, misused, and overused. It should probably be struck from the language. When an old man forgets his hat, he is called senile. When a young man does the same thing, he is called forgetful. Such is ageism, which (like other prejudices) uses the double bind with impunity. For fear of being labeled senile if they make mistakes, older people may avoid seeking new skills or taking tests in old ones. They are then labeled rigid, lacking in curiosity, and resistant to change.

The truth is that much of what has been called aging is really the result of overmedication or physical disorders such as atherosclerosis or infections. In one study, mental and physical functions of healthy men with an average age of seventy-four compared favorably with those whose average age was twenty-one. Some slowing of response was found, but this correlated with environmental deprivation and depression as well as with age.[8]

One of the sadder things that ageism has done is to deny the older person his or her sexuality. There are a few physical changes with age that bear on sexual function: a need for somewhat more direct stimulation for arousal in the man, and a tendency toward vaginal dryness in the woman, especially if sexual activity is interrupted for an extended period of time. These changes pale in comparison to the damage done to the older person's sense of self-worth by ageism's implication that sex in old age is silly, dirty, or bad. Don't believe it! We come into this world as physical, sensual, sexual beings, and we leave it the same way.

Social Aspects of Ageism

Think now about some of the social aspects of ageism. The major social problems you face today involve society's definition of your role, or, more precisely, lack of role. Not having society telling you who to be and how to be it can be an advantage, especially if you're the kind of person who prefers a more free-form, inner-directed life. But the very lack of clarity that allows for individual choices may also lead to bewilderment and frustration. You may end up feeling too old to work, too young to die, and unable to find a satisfactory balance in the middle.

Remember that no one else exactly like you has ever been old before. Therefore, no one else can really know what is right for you in this phase of your life. It is your life and your decision. In fact, one of the rewards of later life may be that you are less restrained by strict role definitions. Perhaps this is a natural outgrowth of the aging process itself, designed to allow you to use the knowledge and experience of a lifetime to grow and develop, to become fulfilled as a human being.

Consider the social position of the older person in America—the way you are perceived by others and yourself. A lot of erroneous information has been carried over in a historical sense, and the prejudice of ageism sometimes prevents reexamination of the facts. Older people became socially disadvantaged relative to the young during the period between the world wars, with migration into urban centers, decreased self-employment, mandatory retirement practices, changes in the composition of the family, and a general aging of the population. Such trends contributed to social isolation, decreased participation in the labor force, lower income, financial dissatisfaction, and poorer health. But has the position of the older person in today's society continued downward? Definitely not!

The number of older people in the labor force has decreased since World War II, but this is largely because of voluntary retirement. Only one in ten people are now obliged to retire.[9] Most people who have the option elect early retirement. Income is higher, health is better, and older people report overall satisfaction with both health and income. Most people don't feel isolated in later life. Though more older people now live alone or with unrelated others than live with adult children, this arrangement is by choice, and it is made possible by improved financial status.[10]

Serious social inequities still exist, especially for older women and minorities. But knowledge of this more positive trend may help you to avoid the dread and decrease the paralyzing stigma of old age in our society.

Retirement may be seen as a prototypical social issue of ageism. The myth goes something like this: "Once retired, older persons are finally able to enjoy life fully, without the pressures of day-to-day living."[11] But what is life if it is not day-to-day living? While it is true that some people look forward to retirement, others would prefer to continue what for them is productive and fulfilling work. Ageism denies the right to choose.

Freedom to choose also means freedom to choose retirement. If, for example, you find your job boring or backbreaking, you may look forward to starting over. You may not dread retirement at all. The women's movement illustrates the importance of choices. In the early days, so strong was the desire to eliminate the stereotypes that the very word "housewife" took on negative connotations. But today, fair-minded people have come to realize that real freedom means freedom to choose a traditional role as well.

The same options should apply to retirement. Not all older people may wish to stay on the job or to join the Gray Panthers to fight ageism, but the choice should be available.

Perhaps, at least as long as society persists in demanding retirement at some arbitrarily determined age, you would do well to look upon retirement as a beginning rather than an end—the beginning of later life. The social components of ageism are best fought by getting and using the facts to deny the stereotypes. As an older person, you deserve respect, dignity, and the right to set up your life as you see fit.

Psychological Aspects of Ageism

Because any prejudice is a mental invention, it may seem redundant to speak of the psychological aspects of ageism. In considering its biological and social weapons, you have already learned about the first-degree crimes of ageism: isolation, loss of freedom, and decreased sense of personal worth. These are obviously important in the psychological makeup of the older person. But the most damaging myth of ageism is whichever of these you believe enough to allow it to hurt you, to stop you from selecting and shaping for yourself the kind of life you want. Simple fear of the unknown, or of specific biological, social, or psychological changes, may be enough to precipitate depression, anxiety, or frustration.

At all ages of human life, adaptability is the most important psychological trait, and it depends on physical and mental health, individual personality, earlier life experience, and interpersonal support systems. One of the reasons you have reached older age is that you are a survivor. Remember that the next time anyone tries to ignore you or put you down because of your age!

How does ageism, with its biological, psychological, and social myths affect you as you try to plan for retirement and later life? There is prejudice in the job market, some subtle and some fairly blatant. You may face this if you decide to bolster your budget by working after retirement. You may face it if you decide to stay on the job rather than retire. You may find yourself devalued by people who do not look beyond your years to the person you are.

Ageism exists because people are afraid of getting older, afraid of sickness, of death, of being different. Ironically, that fear tends to promote avoidance of real contact by younger people with older people, thereby increasing the opportunity for misunderstanding. More ageism and more fear follow.

In the long run, the worst thing about prejudice is that an entire group of people is denied options and personal freedom. As long as ageism is in force, our society remains biased, and the people in it continue to dread old age. There is demoralization and devaluation. People do not plan for their later years, in the mistaken belief that they have no options. Later life is not satisfactory, and a vicious cycle of self-fulfilling prophecies and unhappiness ensues.

You can make a difference. You are in the process of doing so right now. You are learning the facts, looking at your options, and planning. The stereotypes will yield to the facts and to the human beings who face them with dignity and courage. You will have scored a victory for yourself and the future every time you follow your own heart and mind as you plot your course through later life.

Attitude

While ageism is a sociocultural phenomenon, attitude is individual. Yes, attitude is often influenced by the society in which you live. But society doesn't suffer (except in the long-term sense of wasted resources) if *you* believe and act in accordance with the negative stereotypes and devaluation of ageism. You do if you are pushed out of work you love strictly on the basis of your age; if you don't take the computer class at the university because you think you're too old; or if you spend most of your time worrying about when the "inevitable" senility or debilitation is going to strike.

These are the tragedies of ageism brought home—the loss of fulfillment, the unnecessary dread and anxiety, the waste of a valuable human life. *Your attitude is the key to staying out of the prison that is age prejudice.*

Think back to when you were twenty-five or thirty years old. Did you think of aging? How about retirement? What was your attitude then? Has it changed? Younger workers often have generally positive attitudes toward retirement, but little or no factual information about where their money will come from, how they will spend their time, or how it might affect their health or relationships. On the other hand, when asked what it's like to be old, younger people tend to greatly overestimate problems with loneliness, boredom, job opportunities, or health.

Older people hold more negative attitudes toward retirement, partly for specific financial, health, or relationship reasons, and partly because there is a vague sense of dread surrounding the process. Conversely, attitudes toward aging have become more positive by this time, with fewer than 10 percent of older people reporting serious problems with loneliness, boredom, job opportunities, or health.[12] Many of these same older people, however, also say they believe themselves to be exceptions to the general rule of unhappiness and ill health in old age. Such is the power of attitude—that it can remain unexamined and unchanged regardless of the facts or lack thereof.

Look at how these inaccurate attitudes discourage planning. If at thirty years old you believe that you will be worthless at sixty or eighty, you are not likely to plan for that time in your life or to look forward to it. You are less likely to fully explore your options and more prone to give up on being fulfilled and satisfied when you are older. Your self-esteem, based as it is on chronological youth, is bound to erode. You may find yourself prejudiced against yourself. If at sixty or eighty you believe that you are the exception to the rule of ineffectiveness and unhappiness in old age, you may tend to think yourself privileged rather than simply continuing your life in a normal, healthy way. Such an attitude can incline you toward being careful all the time, never stretching yourself, always "walking on eggs," afraid you'll upset the precarious grip you have on life as one of the "lucky few" older people.

For you and society, then, there is an information gap to be overcome before each person, regardless of age, can be considered worthwhile, capable, and entitled to continued challenges and satisfaction in life. Because we grow into old age thinking that something is supposed to be wrong with us when we get there, we are often inordinately surprised to find that we stay about the same, with the same strengths and weaknesses, desires and fears.

You do not have to give way to the cruelty and injustice of ageism. You are now taking charge of your own attitude. You are learning about healthy aging, keeping it separate enough from other related events to allow yourself freedom and choice. These are the important lessons of the three As, lessons that can be used in four ways:

1. *Get the facts*—information about normal, healthy aging is more than a match for the myth and foolishness of ageism. There are some biological changes with age, but these are not generally as limiting as the rigid and inaccurate cultural stereotypes might make you think. You can prevent, minimize, or cope with any problems that arise, just like at any other age. Armed with knowledge, you can look for solutions instead of accepting whatever comes your way as simply your lot.

2. *Share these facts with others*—friends, family, employers, employees, even congressional representatives. In the long run, this is how society changes. Yes, it's agonizingly slow at times, and the changes often happen too late to help those who worked hardest to bring them about, but you'll gain satisfaction and a feeling of connectedness with coming generations. You'll have done some good for others in their later years.

3. *Know yourself*—your fears and weaknesses, your strengths and abilities, your resources and liabilities, your expectations and goals. Only with this knowledge of yourself can you tailor a plan for a good old age. *Trust yourself.* If you feel conflict about going against some cultural stereotype, say to yourself, "I am a unique person with my own unique strengths and weaknesses, needs and abilities. No one exactly like me has ever been old before, so I can decide what is right for me." Stay aware that you have choices, that options are not closed to you simply on the basis of the number of years you have lived.

4. *Use your knowledge* about aging, about ageism and the obstacles it

is likely to throw your way, about yourself, and about your own attitudes to *plan,* to meet your own goals for later life. You are entering another stage of development along life's continuum, one that offers new opportunities for personal enrichment and growth. Don't retire from life just because you've lived some years already. There are more to come—yours to use and enjoy.

Notes

1. A. Comfort, "Age Prejudice in America," in *Older Persons: Unused Resources for Unmet Needs,* ed. F. Reissman (Beverly Hills: Sage Publications, 1977).

2. M. Clark and B. G. Anderson, *Culture and Aging: An Anthropological Study of Older Americans* (Springfield, Ill.: Charles C. Thomas, 1967).

3. H. Estes, "Health experience in the elderly," in *Dimensions of Aging: Readings,* eds. J. Hendricks and C. D. Hendricks (Cambridge, Mass.: Winthrop Publishers, Inc., 1979).

4. A. Comfort, *A Good Age* (New York: Crown Publishers, Inc., 1976). This is recommended reading.

5. R. N. Butler and M. I. Lewis, *Aging and Mental Health: Positive Psychosocial Approaches,* 2d ed. (St. Louis: C. V. Mosky Co., 1977).

6. See note 1 above.

7. See note 5 above.

8. See note 5 above.

9. R. C. Atchley, *The Social Forces in Later Life: An Introduction to Social Gerontology* (Belmont, Calif.: Wadsworth, 1972).

10. F. C. Pampel, *Social Change and the Aged: Recent Trends in the United States* (Lexington, Mass. and Toronto: Lexington Books, D.C. Heath & Co., 1981).

11. J. C. Morgan, *Becoming Old: An Introduction to Social Gerontology,* vol. 3 in the Springer Series on Adulthood and Aging (New York: Springer Publishing Co., 1979).

12. See note 9 above.

Part 2

Decisions

5 What Kind of Later Life Do You Want?

1. Avoid fried meats, which angry up the blood.
2. If your stomach disputes you, lie down and pacify it with cool thoughts.
3. Keep the juices flowing by jangling around gently as you move.
4. Go very light on the vices, such as carrying on in society. The social rumble ain't restful.
5. Avoid running at all times.
6. Don't look back. Something might be gaining on you.

—Satchel Paige's six rules

One of the reasons retirement has a bad reputation is that sometimes people with "hidden" problems seem to fall apart after they retire. It's logical to blame the problem on retirement, then, right? But think about it a little more. Does retirement itself do something harmful? Probably not. More likely, the person whose problems are "unmasked" by retirement suffers because his or her job filled needs that are not being met after retirement. That's why you should think about what kind of later life you want.

What will you do with your time? Notice that I didn't ask what you were going to do with your time after retirement. That's because the implications are different. If you only think of planning how you will spend your time after you *retire*, you have already mentally limited your planning options by *assuming* you will retire. You are at the mercy of this "beast"—obviously not a way to feel confident and competent as you approach your later life.

In the field of mental health, a great deal of effort is expended to help people get the right amount of "structure" in their lives. Patients are felt to require hospitalization at times to impose order and structure, to live in group homes to maintain it, and to arrange their days to include it. In this sense, "structure" means organized time. And, for the most part, organized time means activities.

The trouble with saying that you need activities in later life is that it tends to promote degrading stereotypes of older people as unproductive people who are filling time with a lot of meaningless motion. In Hemingway's phrase, that's confusing movement with action. You don't need that. What you need is activity in the singular—a purpose, something that occupies you, challenges you, fulfills you, gives you good reason to get up in the morning. This is "life work," described by Ueland as "anything you love and want to do or to make. It may be a six-act tragedy in blank verse, it may be dressmaking or acrobatics, or inventing a new system of double-entry bookkeeping. But you must be *sure* that your imagination and love are behind it, that you are not working just from grim resolutions."[1]

Basic personality does not change with age. If you're an active person with many interests at age thirty, you will likely be so at fifty and eighty. If you are happy with a more sedate lifestyle in your younger years, you will probably feel most comfortable with a similar lifestyle in your sixties and seventies. The needs you have now will be with you later. The life with which you are comfortable now is the life you'll like in the future.

To get where you want to go, you have to know where you are. You need a map, complete with an arrow labeled, "You are here!" Similarly, to get the kind of later life you want, you must know yourself and your needs. The worksheets at the end of this chapter are designed to help you determine where you are, so you can figure out where you want to go—to draw a map for your later life. Work through each one carefully before proceeding to the next. Allow yourself plenty of time to really think about the questions.

The way people arrange their lives is usually no accident. Consciously or not, you have probably set things up a certain way because that way either satisfies you or protects you. Look for clues in how you feel about what you do. For example, you may involve yourself in a lot of activities at work because these activities genuinely make you feel good about yourself and your place in the world. On the other hand, perhaps you use the "busy defense." Maybe your relationships with others don't turn out as you'd like, or you feel empty and unproductive, so you fill your hours "doing things" to cover up your pain and loneliness.

On the other hand, if your activity is low, maybe you keep it that way because you don't feel good enough about yourself to risk trying new things. You need all your energy just to make it through the day. Conversely, perhaps a lower level of activity fits your style. You like to take your time with what you do and you enjoy allowing room in your schedule for doing whatever comes to mind at the moment.

What you do with your time has meaning for you and the people around you. Understanding this meaning allows you to plan for getting the most out of your later life. Your next step is to decide whether you want to change or maintain your current activity patterns. Activity Worksheets 5.1–5.3 (pp. 58–65) will help you determine your *own* patterns.

The Eight Activity Patterns

To get more specific about what kind of later life you want, first think about your goals. Maybe you want to travel or learn a language. Maybe you've watched your eighteen-year-old daughter go out your door on her way to college, and realized with sadness that you hardly know her. Perhaps you want to spend more time with the important people in your life. It's time to make some decisions.

As you read, write in the margin—your ideas, goals, plans, things you want to discuss with other people. Don't stop to criticize yourself. Just write down your thoughts, no matter how "impractical" or "illogical." You can work out the details later; neatness doesn't count now. What you are after here is energy and ideas, so scribble away—the more the better!

Pattern 1:
High-Activity—Highly Work-Oriented—Satisfied

You are an active person, and your activity centers around your work. You have the kind of energy that makes planning and taking on new tasks easier. That's an advantage. You have established a pattern of life that satisfies you. That's also an advantage, since people who find ways to be happy and fulfilled at one point in their lives can usually do the same at other stages.

Remember that you have established this pattern of activity because it suits you. Now consider what you want from your later life. Do you want to maintain the same pattern or are there things you want to change? The question of whether or not to retire is an important one for you because of your emphasis on work. If you retire, be careful to plan your later life to be sufficiently active and stimulated—intellectually, physically, socially, and emotionally. You are not the kind of person who is likely to do well in a rocking chair on the porch.

The major problem you face, especially if you retire, is that you do not have many activities outside of work. Start now by thinking of some other things you might like to do. Review the activity worksheets for ideas. If you need help, there is a list of Activity Options at the end of this chapter, arranged from high to low activity. Because of your tendency to prefer an active life, you may want to concentrate on some of the things at the top of the list.

Give serious thought to continuing your work if that is your preference and you have the option. But the transition into later life can provide you with the opportunity to make some changes as well. Think about ways to achieve a balance between work and play. Or perhaps you want to modify your work—enter a new area or begin some new projects. Be sure to consider your personal life. Do your relationships need work? Is your emotional life satisfactory? Now is the time to reassess. Later life is yours to enjoy. Make the most of it!

Pattern 2:
High-Activity—Less Work-Oriented—Satisfied

You are active and generally satisfied with the pattern of your life. You also have interests and pursuits outside of your work. This is one of the most easily adapted positions for later life. Part of your strength lies in the fact that you have already developed a pattern of activity that satisfies your basic needs and wants. ("If it ain't broke, don't fix it," the saying goes.) If you retire, the transition is likely to be smooth because you are ready to replace work with other activities.

Because your activities are based on a variety of interests, your pattern of life, both now and later, is apt to be more balanced than that of someone whose focus is primarily and intensely on work. But be sure to review your activity worksheets to look for areas where you might want to make changes. Transition periods such as retirement and moving into later life can provide you with opportunities for growth and development of different parts of yourself. For some other ideas for development, review the Activity Options list at the end of this chapter.

If you're in this activity group, don't let your current satisfaction prevent you from thinking about what you would do if something happened to change your plans. Some people have problems adjusting to later life because they get overwhelmed by unexpected events. For example, what would you do with your life if you lost your spouse or developed severe health problems? You certainly don't have to go looking for trouble, but it doesn't hurt to think of some "standby" options.

You are energetic and resourceful. You have a variety of interests. You know what satisfies you, and you have been able to achieve that satisfaction. You are therefore well equipped to get the kind of later life you want. Start now. Think about your goals. Prepare for any problems you can foresee. You have some later living to do!

Pattern 3:
High-Activity—Highly Work-Oriented—Unsatisfied

Your activity is high and strongly work-oriented. For some reason you are unsatisfied with it, however. Perhaps your life is not balanced. Maybe you spend too much time at work and not enough in rejuvenating play. Maybe your relationships with other people are troubled or you schedule yourself so tightly that you hardly have time to catch your breath each day, much less to pursue any outside interests.

Your task is a bit more complicated than that of someone who has already attained a satisfactory pattern of activity. You need to change, not just maintain.

The first problem you face is to ascertain the source of your dissatisfaction. If you retire, you may have difficulty because there is little in your life besides work. You could become bitter and unhappy, feeling as though you've lost control of your life. Yet some of your dissatisfaction could result from feeling frantic at work instead of challenged and fulfilled. It's as if your life is a tree with work as the only branch—the others were stunted so long ago that there's hardly a bud left. You may already be dissatisfied because of the sense that something is missing. Retirement, at least initially, may only compound the sense of loss unless you make the conscious effort to change. If this is you, look for satisfying nonwork activity; try new things.

Start now by making a wish list. Write down four or five things you have thought you might enjoy. Sometimes people don't do what they really want to do because they can't give themselves "permission" to "waste" time in play when they could be working. Your problem is not that you are lazy. Not only do you deserve time to pursue interests outside of work, but you also need it for optimal later-life satisfaction. See the Time and Feelings Chart (5.2A) to discover what makes you feel good. If you need some ideas, look at the Activity Options list at the end of this chapter. Ask the people who care about you to help. They may know you better than you think! Really *listen* to their suggestions, and *try* some of them.

Your high energy is a strength, and you have been able to channel that energy into your work. Use some of it now to make a more balanced life for yourself. Think of it as a new beginning. Maybe (probably) things won't work out perfectly at first. But remember that it is normal to be nervous when you're learning a new skill. That's no reason to quit. Loosen that stranglehold you have on yourself and get started. It's never too late to start growing flowers around the tree of your life.

Pattern 4:
High-Activity—Less Work-Oriented—Unsatisfied

As a highly active person who is less work-oriented but still dissatisfied with your pattern of activity, you have some of the same problems as the person described in the previous category, and you should read about that pattern, too. You may not know the source of your dissatisfaction, but you do have the raw materials (interests outside of work) with which to build a different kind of life. Your tree already has more than one branch, and maybe even a few flowers! That and your relatively high energy level are strengths you can use to transform your later life into something more satisfying.

See Activity Worksheet 5.3 to look for clues to your dissatisfaction. The issue for you may be lack of balance. Or you may be using your activities to escape some empty or unhappy place inside yourself. A Band-Aid on the outside, however, won't fix a hurt on the inside.

Think about the things you do that make you feel good. Can you do more of them? Do you have enough people in your life, and are those relationships strong and fulfilling? If not, start making changes now. It's never too early or too late. Find the source of your dissatisfaction and take action to change. You have the energy and some of the raw materials. Use them to make a better later life for yourself.

Pattern 5:
Low-Activity—Highly Work-Oriented—Satisfied

You are a person with low activity, most of which is work related. You are satisfied with that basic pattern. Your problem is somewhat different from that of the person with a high-activity pattern. For you, the decrease in activity that comes with retirement may be rather welcome. But you still need mental challenge, physical action, being with people, or just relaxation. The particulars vary with the individual, but no one can spend twenty years sleeping, eating, and watching television, without paying for it in terms of diminished self-respect, health, or family relationships.

Your strengths lie in your knowing and having already been able to achieve for yourself the kind of activity pattern you prefer. But people who like a lower level of activity may be surprised, when they retire, to find that they do need some structure time and activities. Since you probably prefer spontaneous activities, and because most of the things you do now are work related, you may not be accustomed to planning your time.

Later life, especially if you retire, gives you the opportunity to organize your life the way you want it. Think about how you spend your time. At first, the decrease in activity brought about by retirement may be welcome, but later time may seem to drag endlessly. Enjoy your new freedom, but think about planning some regular activities. The list of activity options later in this chapter may help you get some ideas. These activities are classified from most activating to least. You may prefer less-activating things in the first few years after you retire, then decide to switch to more-activating ones later. If you don't like to do a lot of planning yourself, think about joining organized groups of people who enjoy the things you do.

In summary, you have the advantage of knowing the kind of activity pattern that suits you, and you are basically satisfied. The major risk for you in planning your later life relates to your not realizing that you need some structure in your life. Because most of your activities are work related, you don't have a lot of other interests to fall back on, and you may not be used to thinking in these terms. Be sure to balance your life—between spontaneous activity and regular, planned activity, between things you do with others and alone, and between sedentary and more-active pursuits. Later life is yours to enjoy.

Pattern 6:
Low-Activity—Less Work-Oriented—Satisfied

As a person who is satisfied with your current activity pattern and whose activities are less work oriented, you are in a good position to make the transition if you retire. You already have some experience with planning rewarding activity outside of work. People who are happy and well adjusted before retirement are most likely to be happy and well adjusted after they retire. The issue for you is how to maintain your satisfactory activity pattern.

Think carefully about what you get from your work. Is that where you get most of your time with other people? If so, you may want to think about planning more social activity after you retire. Does your work challenge you intellectually, in a way that is not replicated by any of your other activities? If so, think about ways to put mental challenge into your later-life activity if you retire. See Activity Worksheets for any unbalanced areas you think might cause problems for you, and plan how you will correct the problem.

Your strength lies in your ability to organize your life as you like it. You know yourself and you have interests and activities in areas other than work. Your basic task is to make sure you replace whatever positive things you lose if you retire, and that you maintain the kind of life that satisfies and fulfills you. Your later life is your own. If you are happy and satisfied with your activity pattern, keep it that way!

Pattern 7:
Low-Activity—Highly Work-Oriented—Unsatisfied

You have a low activity pattern and most of your time is structured at work. For reasons that may not be clear to you, you don't do much except go to work and come home. You haven't developed interests outside of work, and maybe your work is not very satisfying either. Under these circumstances, it's easy to blame the job for taking up all your energy. You may expect things to be different once you retire.

But you'll still be the same person after you retire. Try to determine what the problem has been for you *before* you retire. Why is your work unsatisfying? Why have you no other interests? Perhaps you have been depressed or physically ill. Maybe you have trouble getting organized or are afraid to try something new. Whatever your problem, you can be sure that it won't magically disappear once you retire. You will have to work at overcoming it, to develop a new pattern of activities and interests.

Start now. Review your Activity Worksheets. Can you see where the difficulty might be? Assuming your low activity pattern is not the result of depression or other illness of some kind (less likely to be the case if the pattern is lifelong), the issue for you may be one of balance, or of being timid about exploring new things.

Think of later life as a time to reassess and start over. Make a wish list. Did you ever watch a group of people playing volleyball on the beach and wish you could join them? What was it that attracted you to them? The pleasure of the game? Their happy camaraderie? Write it down and think of how you can get that involvement for yourself. Expect some trial and error. After all, you are trying to change a long-standing pattern. Maybe the first few tries won't work well. So what? You'll be expanding and growing—living your life in the moment instead of measuring it out on someone else's yardstick!

For ideas of what to do, see the list of Activity Options at the end of this chapter. Some things are more activating than others. Be realistic and set yourself up for success. Instead of starting out by making plans for a new career (*very* activating), begin more modestly, such as by joining a club or organization that structures activities around something that interests you. Change can be difficult at first; give yourself every opportunity to succeed. New things are done with difficulty before they're done with ease, so don't be critical of yourself for starting small. You're starting. That, plus not giving up, means you'll get there.

Pattern 8:
Low-Activity—Less Work-Oriented—Unsatisfied

You have a low-activity, less work-oriented pattern, with which you are unsatisfied. You do have other activities to "plug into" once the structure of work is no longer available if you retire. That's a strength. But there is something about the pattern of your life that does not satisfy you. Using your Activity Worksheets, can you identify what's wrong?

Your low activity, if it is a lifelong pattern, probably is not the problem. You have that pattern for a reason. The difficulty may actually translate into a question of balance between what you want to do and what you actually are doing. But you have an asset—your interests outside of work. They can be building blocks on which you can base a new pattern of activity in later life.

Consider, for example, a person who undergoes cosmetic surgery or someone who loses a great deal of weight. He or she may be disappointed that life is not drastically different after the surgery or the weight loss. Such disappointments often result from unrealistic expectations. You're still the same person underneath, whether you weigh 250 pounds or 150, whether you have your nose fixed or not, before and after you retire. You have the same strengths and weaknesses, the same outlook on life, the same capacity for change and growth.

Your advantage, as you plan for later life, is that you have the opportunity to realize some of your potential for change and growth. Of course that potential is always there at any time of your life, but transition points can promote reevaluation and support a firm resolve to make things different. Entering later life is just such a transition point. Check the feelings noted in your Activity Worksheets. When do you feel happy and at peace with yourself? Is it when you work in your yard? When you talk to people at work? When you read a new book?

After you've discovered the things that make you feel good, start planning ways to incorporate these things into your life more regularly. Do it now. Don't wait until after you retire. Transitions are easier if you approach them gradually. You're trying to change your activity pattern, not just maintain the one you have. You might try several things before you find the lifestyle that suits you. That's okay. You will be making progress with every new thing you try, and making changes takes time and effort. Congratulate yourself on your successes and don't dwell on your difficulties.

A story may help you remember this lesson: An accomplished surgeon trained young doctors fresh out of medical school in the art and practice of surgery. Often his nervous students were slow at their work, fumbling anxiously as they tried to swiftly complete the complicated surgical techniques with their teacher's finesse and skill. At such times, exasperated with the awkward efforts of the young trainees, the old doctor would roll his eyes to the heavens and intone dramatically, "Little steps for little feet." Then, the air cleared, they would return, teacher and students, to the task at hand. Allow yourself to fumble a bit as you work on your plan for later life. You can do it.

Transition and Balance

How can you get the most from your later life? Early theories promoted keeping busy—the busier the better. More recent thinking promotes gradual "disengagement" as the "normal" way to age.[2]

Human beings, however, are an incorrigibly complicated lot, forever thwarting the efforts of careful scientists to categorize them into this or that neat little statistical niche. The available evidence just does not support the idea that everyone has to be either very active or very content to remain passive in order to adjust well in later life. Successfully adjusted people are not so just by being active, but rather *by pursuing activities that stem from lifelong needs and interests*. Such people are by no means free of inner conflict, but instead develop lifestyles that are continuous with the past. Your later lifetime is there for whatever *you* want to do.

Retirement is a transition point, a time of reassessment after which some roles can be dropped and others embraced with renewed vigor. What you do and don't do—how you choose to live your later life— are individual matters. Granted, work is often a central role, but it is by no means the only thing that defines you as a person, either to yourself or to the outside world. In fact, when work is virtually the only organizing force in life, maladjustment to retirement becomes a real risk.

Balance is critical in making your plan for later-life activity. There must be balance between acceptance of whatever changes come your way with age and recognition of yourself as a valuable person who deserves satisfying activity, respect, and autonomy; between work and play; between independence and the fulfilling mutual dependence of good relationships with others; and between the roles you leave behind and the new ones you establish.

When things are out of balance, there is a mismatch between what you need and what you get, which increases your potential for poor adjustment.

You can achieve balance because you have options. People who perceive themselves as generally in control of events and activities in their lives tend to adjust more easily to the things that happen to them. In psychological terms, this is called having an "internal locus of control." By contrast, people with an "external locus of control" tend to feel at the mercy of outside forces and circumstances. One way to feel in control is to plan for how you will spend your time and get your needs met. That is what you're doing right now.

Whatever kind of later life you want, you have certain basic needs: to feel useful, to help others, to have friends, to stay mentally alert, to keep healthy and physically active, and to relax. These are the things most people say they want from life after they retire.[3] Sounds like what anyone might want at any time in life, doesn't it? And that is precisely the point. You do not suddenly stop needing the things that give you a positive sense of yourself by virtue of having lived or worked a certain number of years. What you do with your time is not important just for its own sake, but as a reflection of your sense of yourself as an alive, interesting, and productive person.

A strong, healthy, positive regard for yourself as you *really* are is crucial in making a good adjustment to later life. In fact, self-esteem and self-respect derive from this at all points in your life. That is why it's such a trap to choose your later-life activities from what is generally considered leisure. As Comfort says, "Leisure is a con. It is like being recycled by a shark. . . . Leisure was meant to occupy an occasional afternoon, not twenty years."[4] In the United States, decline of the work ethic and increased emphasis on the importance of developing personal potential and satisfaction have led to increased acceptance of leisure activities as a way to spend your time. That's all well and good, but it's unlikely you'll get much sense of self-esteem from watching television eight hours a day!

More than anyone else, you are responsible for your own role definitions in later life. As a child, your role was relatively dependent on the adults around you. In young and middle adulthood, society has established fairly clear patterns for marriage, family, and work. Even if you haven't always fit the traditional mold, there is still security in knowing what these roles are, and in understanding how you are deviating from them.

In later life, there is little social, cultural, or even individual agreement about the "right" way to be an older person, nor is it clear when and if you are deviating from the "norm."

You can turn the ill-defined roles of later life into an advantage, by deciding which roles you want to play and how you want to play them, regardless of whether or not they fit with what other people think. What you want to avoid is feeling bewildered and helpless in the face of a society that gives you mixed messages about what it wants from you: a society that simultaneously tells you that you can't work anymore and devalues you as unproductive; a society that tells you you're too old to be active and too young to be passive. Forget society. Think about yourself. You may want to slow down in later life. Or you may find such a notion anathema. Or, if you're like most people, you'll find yourself somewhere in the middle. You'll want to give up some roles and take on others, disengage in some areas and engage more actively in others. The choice is yours.

Asking yourself what you will do with your time in later life is a bit like trying to decide, as a teenager, what you want to be when you grow up. You dream and plan and hope and worry: Will I like what I'm doing? Will I succeed? Is it practical? Am I selling myself short? What will other people think?

The fact is that, whether you're a teenager or a bit older, most of these questions don't make a particle of difference. What counts is that you feel involved and interested in what you do. That you get up in the morning looking forward to what the day will bring. The particulars of what you are doing—learning to speak French, writing a play, building a business, making a quilt, going to work as usual, or sitting on the porch with your grandson—are as important and as unimportant as what you do at any other time in your life. Whatever you do, the key is not to give up on yourself and act like you already are dead and buried. You are growing and changing. You are living. Your first plan may give way to others, which may then lead you down another path. That's the nature of life lived fully in the moment—what Carlos Castaneda called the "path with heart."

Things to Think About

1. Do you want to maintain the same general pattern of activity you have now?

2. Can you foresee potential problems with keeping things the same? What are they? What are some ways you can begin to deal with or prevent these problems now?

3. Do you want to make some changes in the way you spend your time? What are they? How can you begin planning for these changes now?

4. What would be the ideal daily routine for you? Can you start working toward it now?

5. Do you need some ideas for ways to increase or maintain your activity level? See the Activity Options List to get started. Write down some things you might like to add to your life.

6. Is your life balanced between work and play? Between solitary time and time with others? Between active and sedentary pursuits? What do you do for others? What do you do just for yourself? What has intellectual challenges? What is just plain fun? What can you do now to achieve a better balance in these areas?

Notes

1. B. Ueland, *If You Want to Write . . . .*, 2nd ed. (St. Paul: The Schuber Club, 1984). This is recommended reading.

2. W. W. Hunter, *Preparation for Retirement*, 3rd ed., rev. (Ann Arbor, Mich.: Institute of Gerontology, the University of Michigan-Wayne State University, 1976).

3. G. F. Streib, J. Streib, and C. J. Schneider, *Retirement in American Society: Impact and Process* (Ithaca and London: Cornell University Press, 1971).

4. A. Comfort, *A Good Age* (New York: Crown Publishers, Inc., 1976).

ACTIVITY WORKSHEET 5.1
Level of Activity

Examine the following list of paired items and circle the letter above the statement in each pair that fits you best (how you are, not how you'd like to be).

A	B
In an average day, I usually have more things planned than I can actually get done.	In an average day, I usually have an hour or more of free time.
A	**B**
I am the kind of person who feels most comfortable being efficient—the more things I can do at one time, the better.	I am the kind of person who feels most at ease focusing my efforts on one thing at a time.
A	**B**
People often tell me I should slow down, or say they admire my energy and the number of things I get done.	People often tell me to hurry up, or say they admire my calm nature, and the way I am able to protect my free time.
A	**B**
I like to carefully plan how I will spend my time, both at work and play.	I prefer to spend my time spontaneously doing what appeals to me or seems most important at the moment.
A	**B**
I like to do things quickly, and I tend to be grouchy when I have to waste time.	I like to do things at a slow and steady pace, and I tend to be grouchy when rushed.
A	**B**
I don't see how people can just sit around and wait for things to happen.	I don't see how people can race through life without time to think and reflect.
A	**B**
The person I live with (or someone who knows me very well) thinks I'm a high-activity person.*	The person I live with (or someone who knows me very well) thinks I'm a low-activity person.*

(continued)

*Be sure you ask. Partners sometimes can see things about you that you can't see for yourself.

Scoring

Count the number of As and Bs.

If you have more As than Bs, you are generally a *high-activity person*. You often have a lot of things going at once and only rarely do you find yourself with unstructured time in a given week or day.

If you have more Bs than As, you generally organize your life at a slower pace. As a *low-activity person*, you tend to concentrate on one thing at a time, and your activities are often spontaneous and unplanned.

Discussion

Your activity level itself does not determine how well you adjust to retirement and later life. That is, more active people do not automatically do better than less active people. Not everyone needs an eight- to twelve-hour day filled with things to do. Not everyone needs many hours of free time each day. Almost no one needs ten hours of television each day. You need something meaningful to do, but the best level of activity for you depends mostly on you. You need a more specific idea of how you spend your time and how you feel about it. To help you better understand your daily activities, move on to Activity Worksheet 5.2.

ACTIVITY WORKSHEET 5.2
Time and Feelings

This three-page worksheet has two parts: first, a chart on which to record your customary daily activities and your feelings about them, and second, a set of questions to help you analyze what the chart reveals about the way you spend your time. The point of the exercise is to determine how much of your routine activity is work-related, and thus how much "space" in your schedule you will need to replace with other activities when you do retire. It will also permit you to take a close look at things you have been doing, perhaps routinely, for some time and question whether they are satisfying, necessary activities or just habits you have fallen into over time without thinking.

The best method is to keep the chart with you for a full week and, using it as a sort of diary, record as accurately as you can in each slotted block of time both what you have been doing and how you feel about it. Think about each entry and note briefly what you like or dislike about what you have listed. Be sure to include not only actual job responsibilities but all peripheral activities, such as reading, meetings, and social events, that may be regarded as work-related. This will provide the most accurate picture of how much free time you can anticipate once you retire.

Your later life, like all transitions, provides opportunities to grow and develop in new ways. Thinking through what you find most satisfying now in your present routine will give you much insight into how best to direct your time and energy as new opportunities arise in retirement.

(continued)

5.2A Time and Feelings Chart

	6 A.M.– 8 A.M.	8 A.M.– 10 A.M.	10 A.M.– 12 NOON	12 NOON– 2 P.M.	2 P.M.– 4 P.M.	4 P.M.– 6 P.M.	6 P.M.– 8 P.M.	8 P.M.– 10 P.M.	10 P.M.– MIDNIGHT
MONDAY Activity/Feeling									
TUESDAY Activity/Feeling									
WEDNESDAY Activity/Feeling									
THURSDAY Activity/Feeling									
FRIDAY Activity/Feeling									
SATURDAY Activity/Feeling									

(continued)

5.2B Learning from the Time and Feelings Chart

Refer to the chart as often as necessary to answer the following questions:

1. How much of your activity is work-related?

   A. Almost all. I find I have virtually no activities in my life that are not work-related in some way.
   B. Balanced. I spend some time almost every day doing things that are not related to work.
   C. Very little. I spend most of my time in activity unrelated to work.

2. Now look at how you feel about your various activities. List the four things that make you feel best and why you feel that way.

   A.

   B.

   C.

   D.

   (Sample: Working in the garden. I like being outside and working in the warm dirt to make things grow. We always have nice tomatoes and squash to eat, too.)

3. List the four things that make you feel worst and why you feel that way.

   A.

   B.

   C.

   D.

   (Sample: I really hate sorting the mail at work. It's boring, and I'd rather spend time working on the new computer system.)

4. Do you think the way you spend your time is well balanced in terms of:

A. Work and play?	Yes	No
B. Active and sedentary pursuits?	Yes	No
C. Time alone and time with others?	Yes	No
D. Things you do for yourself and things you do for others?	Yes	No

5. If you answered no for any of the paired items in question 4, list the areas you think need work. Alongside each, write two or three ways you can begin to make changes now.

A.

B.

C.

D.

(Sample: I spend too much time alone. I can start to change by going to the game with my brother on Saturdays. Also, renew my membership at the health club. Maybe join a reading club.

Or:

I don't do enough for myself. I can ask the kids for more "time off" from babysitting. Maybe take a class at the university. Get some new clothes.)

ACTIVITY WORKSHEET 5.3
Satisfaction

If you are basically satisfied with your activity pattern, you will probably want to maintain it in later life. If you are unsatisfied, you may want to take this opportunity to make some changes. Your current pattern of activities may not be meeting your needs. The problems, solutions, and implications differ in each case. Use this worksheet to help you make this decision.

Read each of the following statements carefully. Circle yes if the statement seems to accurately describe how you feel, no if it does not.

1. I often feel pressured and without enough time to "just be." **Yes** **No**

2. I think I sometimes use my busy schedule to cover up empty feelings in other areas of my life. **Yes** **No**

3. My relationships with family and friends have suffered, probably as a result of my being constantly "on the go." **Yes** **No**

4. I often feel more frantic than happy or fulfilled by the things I do, as if I'm a slave to my schedule. **Yes** **No**

5. I don't seem to be able to use my time in a way that feels satisfying or productive. **Yes** **No**

6. Because I don't get around to scheduling very many things to do, I think I miss out on some of what life has to offer. **Yes** **No**

7. My relationships with other people have suffered, probably because of my tendency not to get involved as much as I might. **Yes** **No**

8. Instead of feeling relaxed and refreshed after my free time, I often feel down or isolated. **Yes** **No**

9. The amount of time I spend in work-related activity seems out of balance with the time I spend relaxing, being with people, or doing other things. **Yes** **No**

(continued)

64

10. I found one or more areas of imbalance in filling out my Time and Feelings Chart. (See Activity Worksheet 5.2B, question 4.)   **Yes**   **No**

Scoring

If you answered yes to *any* of these questions, your current activity pattern may not be meeting your needs. If you find you have two or more *yes* answers, for the purposes of the discussion that follows, consider yourself *unsatisfied* with your activity pattern.

Discussion

You can now determine your overall activity pattern:

1. From Activity Worksheet 5.1, my activity level is _____ (high or low).

2. From Activity Worksheets 5.2A and 5.2B, my activity is _____ (highly or less highly) work oriented.

3. From Activity Worksheet 5.3, I am _____ (satisfied or unsatisfied) with my activity pattern as it now stands.

Now you can find yourself in one of the eight activity patterns discussed earlier in the chapter (see pp. 47–54). Read the one that applies to you to learn more about specific strengths, potential problems, and suggested planning maneuvers for developing the kind of later life you want. If you are "borderline" in any area, read any patterns that apply.

Activity Options List*

This list is arranged from most to least activating. If you are a high-activity person, for example, you may want to work from the top items. If you are less active or less comfortable with trying new things, you may want to start with some of the bottom alternatives.

More Activating

1. New career (e.g., opening own business)

2. Taking a class/course (e.g., learning a language)

3. Entrepreneurial work (e.g., buying and selling antiques)

4. Continued use of old skills in a new setting (e.g., Peace Corps, or other volunteer work)

5. Part-time work (e.g., temporary, using old or new skills)

6. New leisure or cultural interests (e.g., sport or hobby)

7. New social organizations (e.g., clubs)

Less Activating

*R. M. Belbin, "Retirement strategy in an evolving society," in *Retirement*, ed. F. M. Carp (New York: Behavioral Publications, Inc., 1972).

6 To Retire or Not: Adjustment Is the Question

I think it is all right to work for money, to work to have things enjoyed by people. . . but the mistake is to feel that the work, the effort, the search is not the important and the exciting thing. . . . You should work from now on until you die, with real love and imagination and intelligence, at your writing or whatever work it is that you care about.

—*Brenda Ueland (1891–1985)*

Statistically, most people do retire. Informally, you can tell how common retirement has become in our society by thinking about how rarely you hear the question: *Are* you going to retire? If you are asked at all, the question is usually: *When* are you going to retire?

Consider the difference between these two questions. "Are you going to retire?" implies that you have a choice in the matter, that you will consciously decide one way or the other, based on your own wishes, needs, personality, or life circumstances. To ask "When are you going to retire?" assumes that the real decision, to retire or not, already has been made. It is a foregone conclusion, regardless of what you want or need. It's outside your control.

You have nothing to lose and everything to gain by refusing to accept the premise of that second question. Only one in ten people are forced to retire at a mandatory age; most choose early retirement options. Think of retirement as a *transition point* into a different phase of life. Base your decisions on your own needs, thoughts, and feelings.

Suppose, for example, that you retire with a good plan for managing your later life. You had looked forward to it. Maybe you don't have any extra money, but your days are filled with friends and satisfying activities. Then your husband begins to have memory problems. Over four or five years, these problems become increasingly serious. He leaves the stove burners on and wanders outside at night. You are exhausted from the strain of trying to care for him at home, and you know it can't last much longer. Your doctor tells you that your husband has Alzheimer's disease and gently recommends that you think about a nursing home.

What are you going to do? Money is tight, even with the help you can get from your family and the government. More than that, you're concerned that your life is becoming defined almost completely by your problems. You need something to help you feel positive and productive. You are thinking about going back to work.

Now, in contrast, suppose your situation is the same in every way, except that you don't retire. You don't even think of it, much less plan for it. You like your work, and when your husband's illness first begins, you're thankful you have the work as a social and emotional outlet. And, God knows, the extra money helps. But now things are changing, and you are not sure you want to keep up the pace. You are thinking of retirement, maybe to stay home with your husband and care for him there a little while longer or maybe because you just aren't getting as much out of your work as you once did.

The point of this comparison—with two quite realistic alternatives—is that there are a lot of ways to do things, a lot of "right" ways. People often limit themselves by believing a set of rigid messages about what they should and shouldn't do. Try to think of work and retirement as *options* throughout your later life. Maybe you'd rather retire at sixty-five and do something else at seventy, or retire at seventy-five and not go back to work, or change occupations at sixty-eight and not retire at all. Maybe you'd like to transfer to a new job with the same firm, or change to part-time or temporary work. Do you get the idea? Later life is fluid and dynamic; it is not limited by a lot of "shoulds" and "shouldn'ts," but depends on you.

If you think of retirement as an option, *and only one of many options,* you can see that the decision is best made on the basis of what you know about yourself and what makes you happy. But you may wonder what it's like to adjust to this change.

Adjustment to retirement follows a fairly common sequence: Assuming retirement at age sixty-five, you can expect an initial transition phase of decreased activity, while you settle into the new role. During this time, most people feel generally satisfied with both retirement and later life. Later, often at about age seventy, there is a certain restlessness. You may want to work again, and you're likely to increase your activity. At this point, morale usually improves and people once more feel useful and satisfied with life.[1]

Some people perceive retirement as a loss. If the work you are leaving is an important part of your self-image, you can expect to go through a grieving process if you retire. But if you think of your work as "just a job," this process may be easier. You should know, however, that some people are surprised by how much they miss going to work. This is often the case when work is the center of life and/or there has been little planning.

Adjustment to retirement is a process of change over time. The process starts when you first consider retirement, and abates when your energies have been redistributed into new roles and activities. During that same time period, you may have to adjust to a number of other life changes. Adjustment to retirement depends heavily on the nature of the life changes that result. Your adjustment may therefore vary at different times.

Many studies have not taken duration of retirement into account, and often there is wide variation in how people feel about it. Researchers often report results collectively on groups of people who have been retired for different lengths of time—from as short as two to as long as twenty years. You may not be doing the same things or feel the same way early in your retirement as you do later on.

Surveys of older retired and unemployed people show that as few as 2 percent to as many as 25 percent would like to work.[2] This kind of numerical spread probably indicates the amount of individual variation there is in people's feelings about retirement. Some people seem to fall apart after they retire because the relative lack of structure produces an imbalance in their lives for which they are unable to compensate. Sometimes long-standing troubles have been masked by work. Other people don't seem to need that much structure and are content with lower activity levels. Still others compensate after retirement by pursuing new activities to meet their needs. Clearly, then, adjustment to retirement is an individual matter and depends strongly on your own personality and circumstances.

The Five Adjustment "Types"

Can you predict how hard or easy adjustment to retirement will be for you? A group of researchers has identified two types of people who adjusted poorly and three types who adjusted well in later life.[3] See if you can find yourself in any of these composite "types."

Type 1:
Poor Adjustment—"Angry"

Harry Donaldson retired at age sixty-five, having been in middle management in a large company for most of his career. He was bitter about not having advanced to head of his division, and he felt that certain people "had it in for him" and had actively prevented his promotions. The hiring and subsequent promotion of a number of younger managers with advanced degrees had been particularly upsetting for him, and he had never really felt adequately appreciated, in spite of the competence with which he performed in his position. The thought of growing older filled Mr. Donaldson with dread, so he tried not to think of it at all. He felt emotionally estranged from his wife and children and believed that they did not understand him. His social life was almost nonexistent, and he had made no plans for his retirement.

Mr. Donaldson is an example from the "angry" group—the larger of the two groups of poor adjusters. These people are bitter about not having achieved the goals they set for themselves earlier in life. They tend to blame others for their disappointments and are unable to reconcile themselves to the idea of growing old. Evidence of lifelong personality problems can be seen in troubled relationships with others and difficulty adjusting to change.

Type 2:
Poor Adjustment—"Self-Haters"

Thomas Evans was a teacher. He once had hoped to become principal of his school, but this had never happened, partly due to his limitations as an administrator. He was painfully shy with women and had never married, though he did have one or two female friends, with whom he occasionally shared meals and movies. Mr. Evans sometimes longed for a sense of satisfaction and connection with life but basically viewed himself as incapable of getting either. He saw his life as a disappointment, brought about by his own ineptitude. He was often depressed.

The "self-haters" also look back on their lives with a sense of failure and disappointment. Unlike the "angry" people, however, they tend to blame themselves for this failure. Growing old for them simply means more feelings of inadequacy and low self-worth, and they tend to get depressed. Like the "angry" people, the "self-haters" have usually had adjustment problems earlier in life.

Type 3:
Good Adjustment—"Armored"

Arthur Finney, an engineer with a small electronics firm, wrote out a long list of things to do with his time after he retired and followed a strict schedule of events each day. He did some consulting for his old company, volunteered at the local veteran's hospital, led or served on a number of community affairs committees, took classes at the university, and kept his yard in immaculate condition. He also spent several hours each day jogging, doing calisthenics, and weight training. His biggest fear about growing older was that he might become helpless or dependent, and he especially dreaded the thought of being physically disabled.

"Armored" people such as Mr. Finney don't look forward to retirement or growing older, but their highly developed coping systems function smoothly. They tend to be very active, and the activity has a rather driven quality to it. They cannot face the idea of passivity or helplessness in old age, and their high activity levels protect them from their dread of physical decline. In general, they are afraid of growing old but have strong coping mechanisms.

Type 4:
Good Adjustment—"Rocking Chair"

As a clerk for a large manufacturing company, Lester Garrison was punctual and steady. Others liked him for his ability to remain calm and quiet in the midst of turmoil. In truth, Mr. Garrison did not find that calm particularly difficult to maintain, since his inner attitude was one of detachment when it came to such matters. He was not a very ambitious man, and he was generally satisfied with his lot in life as it afforded him time to spend with a good book in his favorite chair. When he retired, he spent most of his time reading, taking walks, puttering in his rather haphazard garden, and attending whatever social function or visiting whichever grandchild his wife arranged.

"Rocking chair" people are basically passive, and welcome freedom from the responsibilities of their younger lives. They enjoy the extra time and sanction to take care of themselves. They are satisfied with old age, and feel that its advantages in living the passive life they prefer more than compensate for its disadvantages.

Type 5:
Good Adjustment—"Mature"

Gregory Hinton had settled into his job as postal administrator, following a financially disastrous few years in direct sales. He was well liked and capable and had quickly won the trust of most of the other people at his office. He dabbled in real estate and pursued a variety of other interests over the years, making new friends and spending time with his family. He sometimes thought about growing older but figured it would be something he would cope with when the time came.

The mature group is the largest. Relatively free of conflict about self-worth, these people accept themselves realistically and are satisfied with their activities and relationships. Many had adjustment problems when they were younger but feel their lives have been rewarding overall. They can grow old without being overwhelmed with regrets for the past or with fears for the present. They take old age for granted and make the best of it.

There is no "formula" for good adjustment to retirement. If you found yourself among the "good adjusters," congratulations! That will probably make your planning process easier. If you have things in common with the "poor adjusters," remember that most people eventually adjust to retirement.[4]

Don't Panic—Plan!

Some people have trouble adjusting to retirement because it begins so abruptly. One day you're working eight hours and the next day you aren't. Retirement can feel rather final. It is as if once you retire from your current occupation, that's the end of your working life, your meaningful life. Such an arrangement requires people to do something suddenly and irrevocably for which they have almost no preparation and no way to know whether it will suit them or not.

Some companies are trying to keep their valuable and experienced older workers on the job longer. This has advantages to the company of deferring pension payments in addition to a more efficient use of employee resources. Some companies allow employees to ease into retirement or to "try it out." Options such as job sharing and flex-time, without loss of benefits, allow workers to "taper off." One well-known company provides three months of unpaid leave (with benefits intact) to certain employees who are considering retirement. If the employee decides not to retire at the end of the simulated retirement, he or she can go back to work without loss of benefits.

Such plans currently are offered mostly to executives, but you can try negotiating one with your employer. If you do, be sure that all terms are clearly spelled out in a binding formal contract before you leave.

In general, people who retire voluntarily are more likely to feel good about it and adjust faster than those who are forced to retire. The voluntary retirees also tend to have more money, higher occupational status, better health, and more family support. But health status and feeling positive about retirement *before* the event seem to predict satisfaction better than whether the retirement was voluntary or mandatory.[5]

If you are facing mandatory retirement and you don't really want to retire, remember that you still are in control of whether or not you work. Even though you may not be able to continue in the same job, you still have the option of working in some other capacity. Consider your options carefully, and plan a way to maintain the kind of life you prefer.

How well do working women adjust to retirement? This question has not been studied enough to be resolved, but it is clear that if work is important to your self-image, then retirement is a change that requires adjustment, regardless of your gender. Plan for it.

Sometimes things happen in life to interfere with even the best of plans. If you have to retire unexpectedly, you may not have other fulfilling things to do. If you have to go back to work after you retire, you may have to give up some of the other things you wanted to do. If your health fails, you may not be able to pursue some of your former interests. If you lose your spouse, you may not want to continue to follow the same plans. Maybe you don't have the money to do the things you planned or you find that you don't get the satisfaction you anticipated from the plans you made.

If you have difficulty adjusting to retirement or later life, first be sure that you are not sick or depressed. See your doctor if you notice a big change in your energy level, motivation, and enjoyment of life. These can be symptoms of illness or depression, especially if they are new problems for you.

For example, suppose that you are a high-activity person, and that you feel best when you are active. You have always been satisfied with this pattern, and you set up a lot of interesting things to do with your time after retirement. Things go well for the first couple of years. Then you begin to feel less and less like your old self. You just don't have the energy you once had and, over two or three months, you begin to do fewer of your usual activities. You don't sleep well, you lose weight, and you are no longer interested in sex. Life just doesn't seem as interesting. What is wrong with you? Are you "getting old"? Not any faster than you were a few months ago. Have you suddenly become a low-activity person? Not likely.

The changes in the way you feel could be related to any number of physical problems. Or you could be depressed. You need to see your doctor. People who are happy, active, and well adjusted do not suddenly become otherwise without a reason. The problem, whether mental or physical, should be evaluated and treated.

The point to remember is that *adjustment is the norm,* even in difficult circumstances, regardless of your age. If you are ill or having emotional problems, get help. If you lose a loved one, grieve the loss and go on with your life. *Changing your plans does not mean that you have failed.* Go back through this chapter and get some new ideas. Even if you can't change the circumstances of your life, you can most certainly adapt to them. Don't give up. To put it simply, if your first plan for later life doesn't work, make another one!

Things to Think About

1. Do you want or need to retire? Why?
2. Do you want or need to keep working? Why?
3. What might make you change your mind?
4. If you plan to retire, do you want to do it at age sixty-five? Earlier? Later? Why?
5. Have you considered "partial" retirement—continuing to work part-time in some capacity? What are the advantages and disadvantages for you if you choose this option?
6. Have you any past experience with extended unstructured time away from work? How did you fare? Did you enjoy it? Did you settle easily into the new routine? Get bored or restless? Find yourself with ever lower energy? Get overly critical of others?
7. Think about the planning you've done so far. How do you think

retirement will affect your life? Will it be hard for you to adjust? Do the pros outweigh the cons for you?

8. Have any of your friends or family members expressed concern about what will happen if you retire? What are their concerns? Do you think they are justified? Why or why not?

9. Do you think you need some kind of gradual retirement? How can you start to plan it now?

10. Do you think you will have trouble adjusting to retirement? Why? What can you do about it now?

Notes

1. E. Shanas, "Adjustment to retirement: Substitution or accommodation?", in *Retirement,* ed. F. M. Carp (New York: Human Sciences Press, 1972); and M. B. Sussman. "An analytic model for the sociological study of retirement," ibid. See also J. C. Morgan, *Becoming Old: An Introduction to Social Gerontology,* vol. 3 in the Springer Series on Adulthood and Aging (New York: Springer Publishing Co., 1979). See also R. N. Butler, *Why Survive? Being Old in America* (New York; Hagerstown, Md., San Francisco; London: Harper & Row, 1975). This book is recommended reading.

2. R. Stagner, "The affluent society vs. early retirement," *Aging and Work* 1 (1) (1978):25–31.

3. S. Richard, F. Livsom, and P. G. Peterson, "Adjustment to retirement," in *Middle Age and Aging: A Reader in Social Psychology,* ed. B. L. Neugarten (Chicago and London: University of Chicago Press, 1968).

4. J. H. Schultz, *The Economics of Aging* (Belmont, Calif.: Wadsworth, 1976).

5. N. Schmitt, B. W. Coyle, J. Rauschenberger, and J. K. White, "Comparison of early retirees and nonretirees," *Personnel Psychology* 32 (2) (1979): 327–40.

Part 3

Planning

7 Physical Health

We can't take the pain out of the fact that humans aren't immortal or indefinitely disease-proof, or that illnesses accumulate as we age. We can, however, wholly abolish the mischievous idea that after a fixed age we become different, impaired or nonpeople. The start of this demystification has to be in our own rejection of it for ourselves.

—Alexander Comfort in A Good Age

What to Know About
Physical Health in Later Life

Certain things that are obvious in early life need to be clearly and firmly reiterated in later life. How likely is it, for example, that you would hear anyone say that the better your health is at age fifteen, the better your adjustment to high school is likely to be? That statement is certainly true, as indicated by the difficulties experienced by teenagers with physical health problems. But because we assume good physical health in teenagers, its importance is rarely discussed. Contrast this attitude with the situation in later life. The assumption often is made that older people are usually sick or disabled. The result of this assumption is, first, anxiety about getting older and anything connected with it, including retirement. Second is the insidious tendency to believe that, since one is doomed to ill health, there is no point in even trying to improve or maintain physical health at this time in life.

Such assumptions can be hazardous to your health. The facts are that better physical health means easier adjustment to later life; it is not "normal" to be sick or disabled in later life; and you can do things to optimize your health in later life.

Better Health, Better Later Life

Physical health is important at all times in every person's life. An Egyptian proverb says "Health is a crown on a well man's head, only no one can see it but a sick man." The better your physical health, the easier it is to be satisfied and fulfilled. Other things are certainly important, but having your body work properly on most days and in most ways dramatically increases your options. You can go for a brisk walk to clear your head when you feel aggravated or upset. You will take fewer pills and have less chance of developing confusion or physical side effects from these pills. You and your husband can take a trip to see your new grandson. If you run short of money, you can work. Think of your physical health as a precious resource worth your best conservation efforts.

Health care is important to you as an individual and to our society as a whole. Older people make up 10 percent of the population, use 25 percent of the prescription drugs, spend 25–50 percent (estimates vary widely) of the United States health care dollar, occupy 30–60 percent of the acute care hospital beds and 45 percent of the long-term care beds, and take up 40 percent of the average internist's time.[1] In business terms, then, in your later years you are an important "consumer" of this "commodity," and you deserve to be treated accordingly.

Does having health problems mean that you cannot have a satisfactory and fulfilling later life? Absolutely not. It simply means that you may have to work a bit harder at things that are taken for granted by those whose health is better. It may mean that some of your options are more bound by the constraints of your health, or that you need more planning to accomplish some of your goals.

Does the quest for later fulfillment mean you need to ignore or deny your physical health problems and limitations? No. In fact, that would directly contradict the idea that you need to know the facts, face them, and do what you can to make your life better within any constraints imposed by them.

Melvin Quint, for example, felt he had to maintain the appearance of perfect health at all times. At age fifty-five, he was diagnosed as having diabetes severe enough to require the use of insulin, and he spent a great deal of time learning how to give himself the injections at home. But for nearly a year he was repeatedly hospitalized for dangerously high blood sugar. In the hospital, he would rapidly get better on the same doses of medication that had been prescribed before. His general medical doctors were perplexed and frustrated, but their patient remained serene. Finally the psychiatrists were asked to see Mr. Quint in the hope of interrupting the potentially fatal cycle.

To them he revealed the great importance of physical health to his sense of himself. He had been a football star from early school years through college and had continued athletic activities throughout his life. He never had health problems and scorned anyone who "let a little ache or pain" slow them down. Further exploration revealed what his diabetes meant to him and his deeply held belief that anyone who took medicine was "a sick person," who therefore was weak, passive, and dependent. His "solution" to this problem for himself was to "forget" to take his medication.

The appropriate solution, for Mr. Quint and for you, is to understand that the status of your physical health does not completely define you as a person, any more than does your age or your retirement status. The various facts and factors of your life are based on different things. Some are based on choices you make, while some are determined by a combination of luck, heredity, and your own level of preventive maintenance.

Sickness Is Not "Normal" in Later Life

Being sick means feeling terrible, being weak, and having to have other people taking care of you all the time, right? And being old means being sick, right? Nonsense! Besides the fact that it isn't true, there are several problems with saying or believing that it is "normal" to be sick in later life.

The idea gives rise to unnecessary anxiety about the future and contributes to unnecessary dread of getting older.

It promotes a feeling of helplessness that can lead to depression and "giving up" on life.

If you believe that it is "normal" to be sick and disabled when you are older, you may fail to get help for problems that could be treated.

The belief that all older people are sick or senile allows for all sorts of social put-downs, including job discrimination.

Throughout your life so far, what have you been most worried about when you have thought of getting older? "Being sick and disabled" is a common answer to this question. This concern is partly a reflection of the importance of good health to people of all ages. On another level, however, one of the reasons we worry a lot about getting old in this society is that we have been conditioned to believe that "old" is synonymous with "sick." This is not true.

Actually, as an older person you are *less* likely to be affected by acute (short-term) illness, accident, or injury than a younger person, though recovery time may be longer if you do develop such a

problem. From age fifteen to age sixty-five, you are likely to experience
a tenfold increase in the number of chronic (long-term) illnesses you
have. Some of these illnesses will be relatively mild and not at all dis-
abling (such as a bit of arthritis), while some will limit your activity.
Fewer than 1 percent of people over sixty-five, however, are unable to
care for themselves, even though up to 30 percent report some limita-
tion in ability to move around.[2]

If you're like most people, therefore, you can expect to have some
chronic health problems in later life. These problems may limit your
activities mildly or you may need to plan a bit more carefully, but you
certainly need not expect to feel sick or disabled most of the time.
Physical health is no longer (if indeed it ever really was) predictable
solely on the basis of chronological age.

There are three other important concepts for you to understand in
order to be a good guardian of your physical health in later life: (1) the
difference between short-term sickness and chronic illness, (2) the difference between disease and disability, and (3) the difference between
care and cure.

Short-Term Sickness versus Chronic Illness

Short-term sickness refers to things like having the flu or other
infection. It comes on fairly quickly and goes away completely in a
matter of days to weeks. Doctors call this kind of illness "acute." You
generally feel sick in some way, you may need to rest more or have
some help, and you can usually tell when such a problem begins and
ends. Chronic illness is what older people have more often than
younger people. High blood pressure is an example. The start of a
chronic illness may be hard to pinpoint, and your doctor may be the
first to know. The effects continue for months to years and may require lifelong treatment. You may not feel sick or be limited by the
problem except, perhaps, that you need to take medications. The main
difference between short-term sickness and chronic illness is one of
time rather than severity.

Disease versus Disability

Whether the health problem itself is short-term or chronic, there is
a lot of difference between disease and disability. This distinction may
be the physical health factor that most influences how satisfied you
are with your later life. Why? Because the same severity or frequency

of physical disease in two people may lead one to an almost complete inability to function, while the other may find ways to continue to lead a satisfying life. Having a disease does not automatically make you disabled or dependent. Having a physical disability of some kind does not automatically make you helpless or unable to find fulfillment in your life.

Care versus Cure

The science of medicine has mostly been built upon the search for cure, and short-term sicknesses are often amenable to the "quick fix." Antibiotics now can cure infections that once were fatal. But chronic illness is another matter, and the "cure it quick and forget about it" model is not useful. Because of the long time course, interactions with other illnesses, and necessity for coming to terms with the problem emotionally, the model of "care" is much more appropriate. The art of medicine can best be seen here. What can be cured should be cured. What cannot be cured still needs care. The person who has the illness must be attended to, not just the disease or the disability. Emotions must be taken into account, complex combinations of problems must be considered as part of a whole, and judgments must be made that do not neglect the person, the problem, or the situation. Most doctors know this these days, but it is important for you, as an educated "consumer" of health care, to understand these concepts as well.

Remember that it is not "normal" to be sick or disabled in later life. You may need to adapt to some chronic health problems, keeping in mind that disease does not automatically imply disability. You (and your doctor) may need to get used to the idea of care and management for, or adaptation to, some of your health problems. You don't want to spend time, money, and energy chasing *cure* when *care* is what you need, but you do want to get cure when cure is possible. These distinctions may sometimes be difficult, but later life is not the time for rigid concepts or ideas. Physical health is best seen as a continuum—one that is only very generally related to chronological age. Old is not the same as sick.

You Can Maximize Your Health in Later Life

Luck and heredity are only two of the factors that determine health at any age. There are others—factors you can influence. Even if the men in your family for three generations have died of heart attacks, there are still things you can do to give yourself the best chance of a longer, healthier life. Diet, exercise, basic maintenance care, and habits such as smoking and drinking all affect your health in important ways. All are under your control.

Heart disease, cancer, and cerebrovascular disease (strokes) account for about 70 percent of the deaths of people over the age of forty-five. These and most of the other illnesses common in older people are generally chronic rather than acute, and therefore more amenable to prevention and management (care) than to cure. The principles of good health do not change much across the life cycle, but some are more significant or more often problematic in later life. The information that follows is designed to emphasize these principles. This summary isn't designed to take the place of comprehensive care from a good doctor. Use it as a reference. If you need more information, see your doctor.

Some Important Later-Life
Physical Health Issues

Vision

You need the use of your senses to maintain healthy, active contact with the rest of the world. But, with age, most people become less able to see clearly at close range. You may find yourself holding your book or newspaper farther and farther away. In other words, "There's nothing wrong with my eyes. It's just that my arms are too short." This problem is correctable with glasses.

Blindness in later life is relatively uncommon and usually preventable. The most common causes are cataracts and glaucoma. A cataract is a clouding of the lens of the eye, but fortunately this is surgically correctable. One older patient exclaimed in delight after his cataracts were removed, "Well, I'll be damned! There's a second hand on this watch!"

Glaucoma results when the fluid drainage system in the eye fails to work properly and the pressure damages the big nerve responsible for vision. It is painless and without any other symptoms at first, but medical and surgical treatments are effective in preventing blindness, and the problem is easily diagnosed with routine testing. Cataracts, glaucoma, and many other problems can be treated, but only if diagnosed. Get regular eye checkups.

Hearing

Hearing loss is much more common in later life than loss of vision and can leave you out of touch with the world around you. This isolation can lead to depression and even paranoia at times. Most of the loss is of the higher pitched sounds, which unfortunately are important in understanding normal speech. About 5 percent of people over fifty years old and about 25 percent of those over seventy-five have some noticeable hearing loss.[3] Some forms of hearing loss are successfully treated with hearing aids, while others are not. You will not know which kind you have until you are tested. Be sure that you have this done at a reputable hospital or by a specialist your doctor recommends. Many people have been conned out of large sums of money for bogus testing and worthless "cures."

Sex

The myths in our society about aging and sexuality have been very damaging. There is absolutely no reason why healthy older people cannot have enjoyable sex lives. Men may need more direct stimulation to get an erection, and health problems such as hardening of the arteries, diabetes, and some medications can interfere. Alcohol and anxiety about performance can be detrimental in older (as well as younger) men. Women may have no physical changes unless they are sexually abstinent for a long time, in which case the vagina may become tight and lubrication slower. Use a lubricating agent if you need one. For both men and women, masturbation can be a way to maintain your sexual self, even if you are without a regular partner. Use it or lose it!

Nutrition

A healthy diet is a balanced diet and includes fruits, vegetables, grains, and proteins. You should eat chicken and fish more often than red meat and have no more than three eggs per week. Cholesterol, saturated fats, and salt should be kept to a minimum. With a diet like this, there is generally no need for extra (and often expensive) vitamins or other supplements. Calcium for women is an exception, and your doctor may advise specific dietary regimens if you have particular health problems. Brochures and charts are usually available if this is the case.

If you are significantly overweight, a balanced reducing diet is in order. Weight loss and diet changes sometimes can be the only treatment needed for mild high blood pressure or diabetes, and certainly are better than taking medications. A reasonable rate of weight loss is about a pound per week. Aim for the long run, rather than a quick but short-lived change. Your weight reduction program should be geared toward helping you learn new eating habits, and should have you eating "normal" food rather than exotic or expensive groceries.

Common causes of poor nutrition in later years are bad teeth, poorly fitting dentures, and lack of money. Taking care of your own teeth is the best and cheapest way to deal with the first problem. That means regular brushing, flossing, and dental checkups. If you need to wear dentures, make sure they fit well the first time, and take good care of them. Buying food on a tight budget does not have to mean poor nutrition. Shop carefully to decrease waste from spoilage and choose a store where you can buy in quantities appropriate to your needs. Buy fresh fruits and vegetables that are in season, and be aware that modern methods of freezing mean that frozen produce often retains reasonable nutritional value for the price. Use less expensive, leaner cuts of meat or poultry, and remember that you need only three to four ounces of cooked meat, fish, or poultry per serving.

Exercise

Regular exercise is good for your heart, lungs, muscles, and mental well-being. It also helps with weight control. If you do not already exercise regularly, check with your doctor before you begin. You can walk, swim, jog, do aerobics, or lift weights. The important thing is to find a form of exercise that suits your needs and feels good. That way you'll want to do it consistently, at least three times a week. To make sure you *do* exercise regularly, set yourself a schedule or a goal (swimming on Mondays, Wednesdays, and Fridays, or walk 10 miles a week). Exercise may be especially important for you if you just retired from an active job, or if your physical work load has otherwise recently been reduced.

Habits

You can, and should, make some of your biggest health gains in this category. Smoking causes heart disease, lung cancer, and emphysema. You will also get more minor respiratory infections if you smoke and, as you recall, these acute illnesses will cause you more days of limited activity than they did when you were younger. Also, cigarettes are expensive.

Older people may have problems with alcoholism, in spite of all stereotypes to the contrary. Drinking in moderation—an average of no more than one or two beers, mixed drinks, or glasses of wine per day—can be enjoyable. But if you suspect you might have an alcohol problem, get professional help. Be truthful with your doctor about your alcohol use, whether or not you are asked; for your own good, volunteer the information. Alcohol-related questions are sometimes *not* asked by health care professionals because of the mythology that surrounds older people.

Harvey Roberts is a good example. A sixty-three-year-old physician without any prior medical problems, he was in the hospital for minor surgery. Two days after his operation, while recuperating in the hospital, he began to hallucinate and feel bugs crawling on his skin. Shaking and sweating, he didn't know who or where he was. Dr. Roberts nearly died before anyone realized that he was withdrawing from alcohol.

Other forms of drug addiction can create serious mental and physical problems for the older person and may not be easily diagnosed for the same reasons that alcoholism is often missed. Addictions to pain medications or tranquilizers can develop gradually, especially when they are used over long periods of time. Don't be afraid or ashamed to ask for help if you think you need it.

Medications

The older you get, the more likely you are to be taking prescription or nonprescription medications, to be taking more different kinds of medications, and to be at higher risk for adverse side effects and drug interactions. There are basically two medication issues important in later life: taking only what you need to take, and not taking what you don't need to take.

You and your doctor need to be in clear agreement about what medication you are taking and why. You should carry a list of these medications and your medical problems with you, and review it periodically with your doctor. If you see more than one doctor, be sure that each one knows what the others are prescribing, and tell them about whatever nonprescription medications you take. Make sure that the pharmacist always puts the names of your medications on the bottles, and never put one kind of pill into a bottle marked for something else.

No medication will do what it is supposed to do if it sits in a bottle on the bathroom shelf. If you take a number of different medications and have trouble remembering which pill to take when, your pharmacist can give you a small box with compartments labeled for days and times. If arthritis or other problems make it hard for you to get the caps off the bottles, ask the pharmacist to help you devise alternate means of storage.

You can minimize the risk of being harmed by medicines using these simple steps. Start by going through your house from top to bottom, gathering together all the pill bottles you can find. (When I did this on a visit to my grandparents' home, we found some sixty prescription bottles. Some of the pills were in the wrong bottles, some were years past their original prescription dates, and some were not labeled at all.) Throw out anything you can't identify with absolute certainty, anything more than a year old, and anything you are no longer supposed to take.

Bowel Habits

Agnes Sims went to see her doctor because she felt tired all the time. While listing her medications, she casually mentioned that she used laxatives almost every day. When asked why, Mrs. Sims replied that her husband told her that poisons would build up in her body if she didn't have a bowel movement every day. Her tiredness resulted from what was essentially self-induced diarrhea.

You do not have to have a bowel movement every day to be healthy, and the most effective way to "stay regular" is to exercise regularly, drink plenty of water, and eat a diet containing good quantities of natural fiber (fresh fruits and vegetables, bran, etc.) Frequent use of laxatives results in inability of the body to regulate its own function and can cause electrolyte imbalance and dehydration as well.

Everyone has her or his personal bowel rhythm. A persistent change in your usual bowel rhythm, however, can signal more serious problems. Consult your doctor if your normal pattern changes.

Bladder Problems

Prostate gland enlargement is common in older men and may cause your stream of urine to be diminished or hard to start. You may have to get up more frequently to urinate at night. Cancer can also develop in this gland. Prostate problems can easily be detected by your doctor on routine examination. Cancer cells are sometimes found after surgery for an enlarged prostate gland, but this form of cancer can be very slow growing and may not make any difference in your life.

Infections in the urinary tract are more common in women but do occur in older men who have some form of obstruction to the normal flow of urine. The symptoms are increased frequency of and pain during urination. However, infections in older people are notorious for being "silent." That is, when you are older, you may not have the same early warning signs as you might have had when you were younger.

Menopause

When you go through the "change of life," you stop ovulating, no longer have a menstrual period, and then cannot become pregnant. You can still be sexually active and have orgasms. Some women get hot flashes and other uncomfortable physical sensations, especially around the time their cycles become irregular. Hormone replacement may help with these symptoms. You still should have regular gynecologic exams after menopause, however. Vaginal bleeding after menopause may mean cancer of the uterus and should not be ignored.

Pain

There is a big difference between acute and chronic pain. Pain that begins rather suddenly may portend some new physical problem that needs diagnosis and treatment.

Long-standing pain, such as that from arthritis or low back pain, calls for a different approach. Pain medications must be used cautiously and generally should be nonaddictive. It's important for you to learn nonmedical ways of managing chronic pain. If you have a pain problem, be sure you have good referrals to reliable sources for help. There are a lot of bogus operations out there, waiting to separate you from your money by promising cures that do not exist.

Foot Problems

Foot problems are fairly common, can impair your mobility, and therefore affect the quality of your later life. Comfortable, well-fitting shoes are important for both exercise and regular wear. Cut your toenails straight across and not too short. If you have problems, a periodic trip to the podiatrist may be useful. Walking is one of the best ways to exercise and see the world in later life. Keep your feet in good shape.

Atherosclerosis

Hardening of the arteries is related to many of the health problems of later life, including high blood pressure, strokes, and heart disease. Regular exercise, not smoking, and a diet low in cholesterol and saturated fat are preventive measures. Have your blood pressure checked regularly. Report any episodes of dizziness, confusion, numbness, or tingling sensations.

Cancer

There are many kinds of cancer, some rapidly fatal and hard to treat, others slow-growing, easy to diagnose and treat in the early stages, and/or preventable. If you smoke, you should, of course, quit. Women should examine their breasts once a month. Report any unusual swellings or pain, bleeding, unexplained weight loss or fatigue, and change in bowel habits or urinary function. Men and women should have a rectal examination at least yearly and women should also have regular pelvic examinations.

Doctors

If you have ever looked in the yellow pages to find a doctor, you know that the process can be confusing. There are general doctors ("internists" and "family practitioners," for example) and there are specialists—surgeons, psychiatrists, gastroenterologists, gynecologists, neurologists, etc. Now there are also doctors who specialize in working with older people, such as geriatricians and geriatric psychiatrists. How do you choose the right one?

First, you do need a primary doctor, someone to help you keep track of the whole picture of your physical health. This person is most often a *primary care doctor*—an internist or family practitioner. But your primary care doctor could also be a surgeon or other specialist. The important thing is that this person takes care of *you*, not just your heart or your joints or your head. He or she must be willing and able to function as a kind of coordinator of your health care, helping you keep track of your problems and your medications, educating you about preventive measures or alternate forms of care, referring you to specialists when necessary.

Your primary care doctor should be someone who cares for you as a whole person, someone you can trust, someone who can and will take time to talk to you, teach you, get to know you, and work with you. The doctor should be someone who does not subscribe to a lot of ageist myths: in short, someone with whom you have a real relationship—a partnership, in a sense, with the goal of optimal care and management of your physical health in your later years.

Doctors are people. There are good ones and bad ones. Sometimes a perfectly well-qualified doctor may not "match" your personal style. Remember that you have options. Find a doctor you can trust and like, and stick with him or her. If problems develop between you and your physician, discuss your concerns and try to work it out. If you can't work it out, change doctors. You don't want to be "doctor shopping" all the time; it's expensive and it interferes with your medical care. On the other hand, you don't want to stay with someone who doesn't meet your needs.

Finally, remember that you have a role in taking care of your own physical health. Ask questions if you don't understand what your doctor tells you. After all, there is no reason to expect yourself to know all the medical terms. You have a right to clear explanations, in words you understand. There may also be times when you want a second opinion for some reason. That's all right, too. You and your doctor should be able to work as a team to maximize your health in later life.

Planning Better Physical Health
in Later Life

You can start getting healthier anytime—the sooner, the better. Your physical health is one of your most important resources in your mission to have the best later life you can. Any conservation efforts you begin now will help you both now and later. Use the Physical Health Worksheets at the end of this chapter to spur your efforts. If you find problems, have them evaluated by a doctor you can count on.

Coping with Physical Health Issues
in Later Life

If you develop major health problems in later life, it will be necessary to realistically assess yourself and what you want to do. That does not mean you should sell yourself short or set your goals low. But when there are facts to be faced, you must face them. Make a new plan and get on with your life! Consider some examples.

Paul Underwood, a vigorous man in his late fifties, was a computer specialist for a major corporation. He was nearly killed in a serious auto accident, and his injuries required many months of hospitalization for treatment and rehabilitation. As the time of his discharge from the hospital approached, Mr. Underwood became silent and lethargic. He no longer participated in his own care and often asked nurses or family members to do things for him that he had been doing for himself for weeks. As he talked, it became clear that Mr. Underwood had lost faith in his own ability to live independently. He had been hospitalized for so long that he was almost afraid to leave. His adaptation was hampered by the mismatch between what he thought he could do and his actual abilities.

Harriett Vanhorn owns a chain of small specialty-food stores and is exceptionally active in the community and within her family. She is the one who always organizes activities and remembers everyone's birthday. As the pain of her arthritis worsened through the years, she gritted her teeth and refused to give in to it in any way. Many of the activities are no longer fun for her because she is exhausted from the preparations by the time the event arrives, although there are others who could take over some of these tasks. Outwardly she keeps up her image, but inside there is pain and dread for the day when she will no longer by physically able to maintain the facade.

Both of these people have many strengths of character and will, but both had trouble balancing their physical capabilities with their goals and plans. Achieving such balance is not always easy, often because of lifelong beliefs and patterns of behavior. Accurate self-assessment and realistic plans can help.

A certain level of physical well-being would be necessary to move to Hawaii, open a bait-and-tackle shop, and take up surfing, and quite another level to start a bookstore in your neighborhood and print a newsletter on new interpretations of Shakespeare's sonnets. Failure to account accurately for your own resources and limitations can result in two kinds of problems. Like Mr. Underwood, you may underestimate what you can do and miss some satisfying life experiences. Or, like Ms. Vanhorn, you may overestimate what you can do and set yourself up for frustration, depression, and decreased self-esteem.

Coping with Loss

A friend's father says that he wants to die "at the age of ninety-seven, shot by a jealous husband." Most of us can understand that sentiment because it implies death at an old age in vigorous good health, without the prospect of lingering pain and deterioration. The goal of this chapter has been to help you maximize your healthy time. But, despite the advancement of medical knowledge and all of your best efforts to maintain your health, it remains true that everybody has to die of something. Therefore you also need to think about how to cope with death and illness if and when they occur.

There are some general principles about coping with loss that apply for most people whether the loss is of a loved one or of one's own physical health. Knowing these principles may help you to believe that you will adjust, that you will not always feel terrible. There can be comfort in knowing that there is light at the end of the tunnel, even if you can't see it yet. You also will know when to look for help if you get "stuck" and can't seem to adjust to the change.

Let's begin with an example. Barney Waite suffered a stroke that paralyzed his left side. At first he refused to believe he would never regain his former athletic ability. He maintained to his doctors and to his wife that he planned to return to his golf game as soon as he got well. As he worked at his physical therapy and had to face his disability directly, he often became angry and frustrated, flinging his exercise equipment to the floor. This attitude gradually gave way to one of sadness and depression, and Mr. Waite sometimes voiced the opinion that there was very little reason for him to remain alive. But he continued to work at his rehabilitation. As his skills increased, so did his positive mood and self-esteem. He learned to drive again (a car, not a golf ball) and to participate with enjoyment in many of his previous activities. After he was discharged from the hospital, he often returned as a volunteer to talk to other stroke victims about how he had adjusted emotionally and physically to his disability.

This story exemplifies the stages of adjustment to loss. First there is usually a period of **shock and disbelief.** Mr. Waite adamantly disbelieved his condition—he believed he'd recover enough to play golf. Next came **anger** as he, frustrated in his physical therapy exercises, began to believe but not yet to accept. As the disability became real and permanent in his mind, Mr. Waite experienced

sadness. He lingered in this phase for some time and was even mildly suicidal at one point. Finally, however, Mr. Waite was able to accept what had happened to him. He completed his rehabilitation program and continued to cope by helping others in similar situations. This was his **acceptance.**

The four phases of adjustment to loss are overlapping, dynamic, and individually determined. People spend different lengths of time in these stages according to their own personalities, and sometimes people get "stuck" in a particular stage. Mr. Waite had a little trouble with the **sadness** phase, for example. Someone else may feel that it's not right to get angry and therefore have trouble with that phase. Still another person may use drugs or alcohol, dulling the pain of the loss but postponing the completion of the acceptance process.

Severely Debilitating Illness

These adjustment principles hold true whenever you experience a loss. But what if you develop an illness so debilitating that you can no longer make decisions or care for yourself? If, for example, you should have a stroke so profound that you can no longer move, speak, or be aware of your surroundings, how aggressive would you want your medical care to be? Medical technology is so advanced that it is often possible to maintain physical life for relatively long periods of time after the capacities for recovery, enjoyment, and human interaction are lost. Would you want to be maintained on full life support for as long as possible, or not at all?

These are difficult questions to consider, and there are few clearly right or wrong answers. Decisions like this are very painful for family members, and more properly belong with the individual. In years past, doctors were more willing to quietly shoulder some of this responsibility, but in today's legal climate they are likely to discuss with family members the chances of recovery and/or survival without life support. If you have strong feelings about these matters, discuss them carefully with both your family and your doctor. Otherwise, an "all systems go" approach may be taken as long as technology permits, more out of guilt and uncertainty than any real chance of recovery. This heartbreaking scenario is all too common, and the cost is tremendous in both human and financial terms. The specific means by which you can make your wishes known is the living will, a legal document that you can have drawn up by a lawyer, subject to limitations determined by the state in which you live.

Facing Death

From the age of nine or ten, human beings are aware of the finality and inevitability of death, but fear of death tends to peak somewhere between forty and fifty-five. Although some people develop an excessive fear of death that interferes with later life, most older people have accepted the general prospect of dying. Only about 10 percent report strong or marked fear of death.[4]

When a person actually knows that he or she is dying, the responses are similar to the adjustment to loss we saw with the case of Mr. Waite. **Disbelief** is followed by **anger**, which is sometimes expressed toward doctors or family members. At this point there may be **bargaining** with higher powers for a little more time. Next is **sadness**, after which the individual finally experiences **acceptance**. There is often overlapping and shifting from one stage to another, but the process almost always involves these sequential phases.

While the dying person is working through this process, other people must also try to cope with the impending loss. The task is difficult for many people, since it involves recognition of one's own mortality and tolerance of not being able to alter the coming death. Unfortunately, doctors and other medical personnel often don't allow the dying patient to talk about death. Many (80 percent in one study) do not even believe in telling patients the truth about their conditions, because it is "cruel" or "takes away hope." Actually, patients have the right to know (legally and ethically), and more than 80 percent want to be told.[5] You can see, then, that doctors and patients do not think alike on this matter. That's why it's important to express your wishes very clearly *before* any problems develop. What *do* you want to know if you become terminally ill?

Some people find that religious or philosophical beliefs are important in helping them face death. Some want to be sure that funeral arrangements are made in advance and their assets are distributed a certain way, in order to help loved ones cope with the loss. Some want as much control over the time and circumstances of death as possible, and so make use of the living will. A doctor in Los Angeles wrote about the psychotherapy he and his terminally ill wife had during their last year together: "She was learning how to die. I was learning how to live without her. I think we both would have been poorer if she had not been told she was going to die. It was a terrible year, of course, but it was also a year of great love and closeness. If I may use the term, it was a year of greatest beauty."[6] Your death is your own, and whatever you can do to give yourself peace and acceptance is worth doing.

Getting Help

Suppose you develop medical problems with which you cannot seem to cope, in spite of all your efforts and despite the use of all the resources you and your doctor can muster. What then? If you are unable to adjust to changes in your physical health, psychological factors may be interfering. Maybe that will be hard to admit, especially if you have always been able to cope with setbacks when you were younger. Still, the fact remains that adaptation and adjustment are the norm throughout life. People (even doctors) commonly say of someone who has surrendered to a major loss, "That's normal. I'd give up, too." Giving up, however, is *not* the normal human response to stress. There can be a giving-up feeling at times, but in normal adjustment it is temporary.

Fine, you say, but what if it happens? What if I do give up, or I can't adjust? Think back to the reactions of Mr. Waite. Remember his sadness phase? He talked a lot about how pointless the whole rehabilitation process was, and even wondered if life were worth living anymore. But he kept at his exercise program, and he eventually made his adjustment. If he had really given up—stayed stuck in sadness and quit his exercises— he would have had much more difficulty reaching adjustment.

Getting help for medical problems to which you are not adjusting involves two parts. First, be sure that you have not developed new physical problems or complications of the old ones that are making it harder for you to cope. Second, the psychological part of your difficulty coping should be addressed.

Report to your doctor any new symptoms or problems you are having and ask if he or she believes these could be related to any new physical condition. Explain that you are interested in making the best adjustment possible and ask for suggestions. Your doctor may recommend further tests or a second opinion. If you are depressed or having other emotional symptoms, you may be offered referral to a psychiatrist. But sometimes doctors in other specialties are reluctant to suggest such a course of action, for fear you won't accept it. If you're having emotional problems, and your doctor doesn't recommend that you have a mental health evaluation, ask for the referral yourself.

There is no need to postpone getting mental health diagnosis and treatment while your medical workup is in progress.

Sometimes your emotions will talk through your body. Many depressed older people, for example, spend weeks (or months) and a lot of money going from doctor to doctor, getting negative test after negative test, before somebody finally thinks of depression as the culprit. It is sometimes hard to know when a physical symptom is mainly related to an emotional problem, since the body and the mind are inextricably connected. There are always emotional responses to physical disturbances and vice versa. Pain is pain, whether mostly physically or mostly psychologically derived. That is why it's important not to wait to seek mental health care until all the tests are done.

Finally, keep in mind that there are people out there who want to separate you from your money and are willing to trade on your suffering to do so. Some common medical frauds include quack cures for cancer, arthritis, hearing loss, back pain, or loss of memory. If you believe the advertising, there are fountains of youth, vitamins to make you young again, and laxatives that are necessary for your survival. If something sounds too good to be true, it probably is.

A note about paying for health care: Almost all older people in the United States are covered by Medicare, which is a federal program of medical and hospital benefits for recipients of Social Security and their families. It began in 1966 and covers most health care costs, with the important exceptions of outpatient prescriptions and long-term nursing home care. Medicaid, on the other hand, is administered by the individual states and provides health care services for people on welfare. Private insurance covers only 7 percent of the health care expenses of the older population, and many people have been duped into buying expensive, unnecessary, and/or inadequate policies. Know how you will pay for your health care in later life, and be cautious about any policies or programs in which you enroll. For more specific information, check with the office in your state that regulates insurance companies.

Your physical health resources include anything you can use to attain and/or maintain the goal of having your body work well in most ways on most days of your later life. If you have identified problems, discuss them with your doctor and decide on a plan of action. Then get busy and do it! You *can* make a difference for yourself, and it *is* worth the effort!

Things to Think About

1. Better physical health means easier adjustment.
2. Retirement won't kill you or make you sick.
3. It is not "normal" to be sick or disabled in later life.
4. You can maximize your health.
5. Old or young, some people get sick and some do not.
6. People who get sick need evaluation and treatment.
7. If cure is not possible, adjustment almost always is.
8. Failure to adjust necessitates a search for the reason.
9. Older people can and do benefit from medical and psychiatric treatment.

Notes

1. L. S. Libow, "Health care during the retirement years," in *Aging and Retirement: Prospects, Planning, and Policy,* eds. N. G. McClusky and E. P. Borgatta (Beverly Hills and London: Sage Publications, 1981).

2. H. Estes, "Health experience in the elderly," in *Dimensions of Aging: Readings*, eds. J. Hendricks and C. D. Hendricks (Cambridge, Mass.: Winthrop Publishers, Inc., 1979).

3. See note 2 above.

4. M. Puner, *To the Good Long Life: What We Know About Growing Old* (New York: Universe Books, 1974).

5. See note 4 above.

6. See note 4 above.

PHYSICAL HEALTH WORKSHEET 7.1
Checklist

This worksheet is a checklist correlated with some of the things you learned in the first part of this chapter. It is designed to help you identify potential health problems. Review with your doctor any questions or problems you find.

Vision
Have you had to hold your reading farther and farther away?
Has anyone told you that you were squinting?
Have you been given a pressure test for glaucoma this year?

Hearing
Do you frequently ask others to repeat themselves?
Has anyone mentioned that you seem to have trouble hearing?

Sex
Have you noticed any recent changes in your sexual desire?
Have you had problems with getting or keeping an erection?
Have you had vaginal dryness or pain with intercourse?
Do you have orgasms?

Nutrition
Do you understand the basic principles of a healthy diet?
Are you overweight?
If you are on a special diet, do you understand and follow it?
Are your teeth in good condition? Do your dentures fit?

Exercise
Do you exercise at least three times each week?
Have you checked with your doctor about your exercise program?

Habits
Do you smoke or use tobacco in any form?
Do you drink more than two drinks per day (including beer and wine)?
Do you take unprescribed medications?

Bowel Habits
Have you noticed any change in your bowel habits?
Has the color of your bowel movements changed?

(continued)

Bladder Problems

Can you pass urine easily and without pain?
Can you hold your urine if you need to?

Menopause

If you are past the "change of life," have you had any bleeding since then?

Pain

Do you have pain anywhere?
Is the pain old or new?
Do you take any pain medications for it?
Do you ever take prescription medicine more times than as instructed?

Atherosclerosis

Do you know your blood pressure?
Does your heart ever suddenly beat too fast or irregularly?
Do you have chest pain or swelling in your feet and legs?
Do you have headaches or episodes of dizziness?
Do you have episodes of numbness or tingling in your arms or legs?
Do you fall frequently or have trouble with coordination?

Cancer

Have you inexplicably gained or lost weight?
Is your energy level adequate for your usual activities?
Do you have pain, bleeding, or swelling anywhere?
Do you have a persistent sore throat or cough?
Do you check your breasts monthly? get regular pelvic exams?

PHYSICAL HEALTH WORKSHEET 7.2
The Problem List

Suppose you are injured or suddenly get sick and you cannot reach your regular doctor. Could you tell the doctors in the emergency room about your medical problems and your medicines? This worksheet can help you organize important information about your medical problems. If necessary, ask your doctor to help you. (You may even want to put this information on a card in your wallet or pocketbook.)

Problem   **Medications (Name and Dose)**

PHYSICAL HEALTH WORKSHEET 7.3
Medications

For each medication you take, be sure you can answer each of the following questions. Ask your doctor if you need help.

1. What is the name of the medication?

2. What is it for?

3. Exactly how am I supposed to take it (how often, what times of day, relationship to meals or other medications)?

4. How long do I take this medicine?

5. How will I know if I'm taking too much?

6. What are its side effects?

7. Is there a special diet I should have or other measures I could take to reduce my need for the medicine?

8 Mental Health

The diseases of the mind are more destructive than those of the body.

—*Marcus Tullius Cicero (106–43 B.C.)*

The growth of the human mind is still high adventure, in many ways the highest adventure on earth.

—*Norman Cousins*

What to Know about
Mental Health in Later Life

What do you think of when you think about psychiatry? How would you feel about getting help from a psychiatrist? Grace Addison, fifty-eight, came to our clinic for psychotherapy to help her deal with some of her concerns about growing older. For several years she had increasingly worried about the possibility of someday having to depend on others. Fiercely independent, the thought filled her with dread and began to occupy her mind to the point that she had trouble thinking about anything else. In therapy she gradually came to realize that her drive to be independent was based on old fears that the only way she could please others was to take care of them. To her, getting "old and weak," and thus no longer able to care for others, meant that she would be abandoned and alone. In the process of this discovery, Ms. Addison became aware that she also believed herself to be weak because she "couldn't just take care of the problem" herself. It was somehow okay to go to a doctor because of a physical symptom, but going to a doctor for an emotional problem meant admitting to being defective, so she avoided it as long as possible.

Ms. Addison struggled alone with her problem for too long because she had negative feelings about getting mental health care. She is not unique. Many people think of psychiatrists as strange people who give lots of drugs, administer shock treatments, and never talk. They believe

103

that psychiatric care doesn't work, and that having an emotional problem is a sign of personal weakness.

Psychotherapy ("talking therapy"), medications, and even electro-convulsive therapy all are used with success by psychiatrists to treat different kinds of mental health problems. For the older person, the psychiatrist must diagnose the problem, determine the contribution of medical or social problems, and select the best and safest treatment or treatments available. Psychiatric care does work, and having a mental health problem is no more a sign of personal failure than is having a heart attack. A headache hurts whether the cause is tension or bumping your head on a cabinet door, and a person is no less dead from suicide than from a heart attack. You should know about the brain's relationship to the body in order to properly attend to this important part of later life.

Personality

The brain is a marvelously complicated and interesting organ. Its many parts are connected by nerve cells and chemical mechanisms to every part of the body, and the different parts of the brain are all connected to each other. When you slam the car door on your finger, for example, the nerves in your hand almost instantly send a message to your brain, which just as quickly tells you to get your hand out of there.

Then what happens? If you are the kind of person who is stoic about physical pain, you may grit your teeth and stifle your groans until the pain subsides enough for you to go on with what you were doing. On the other hand, if you are not the type to suffer in silence, you may yell out loud, hop up and down, or kick the car. These reactions to slamming your finger in the car door derive from mental mechanisms even more complicated than the ones that first sent the message about the pain in your hand. Such reactions differ between people and are related to *personality*, the unique way of thinking, feeling, and behaving that characterizes a person.

Suppose we carry the example a bit further and say it was your daughter who slammed the door on your hand while you were unloading some groceries. Or your spouse did it, in the middle of an argument about whether or not you were going to a dinner party. Or your two-year-old grandson, who was "helping" with the shopping. Or that obnoxious neighbor who's always lolling about in your yard, wanting to borrow something. Would your reactions be the same in each of these situations? Probably not. Furthermore, in any of these situations, your response would not be exactly the same as anyone else's. It would be uniquely yours.

Where does personality come from? Why are some people charming and others hard to get along with? Why are some people warm and loving, while others are cool and distant? Why are some self-confident and others terrified of making mistakes? There are funny people and serious people, cheerful people and angry people, logical people and emotional people. How did we each get to be the way we are?

The question of whether personality traits derive from biological or psychological and environmental factors has been around for a very long time. It's a trick question, because it wrongly implies that there is an "either-or" answer, that we can separate the mind from the brain, the brain from the body, and the whole self from each of the experiences of a lifetime.

How you live your life is based on your thoughts and feelings, and your thoughts, feelings, and actions combine to make up your personality. This long-standing pattern of thoughts, feelings, and behavior derives partly from innate predispositions and partly from life experiences—nature and nurture. Children who are abused, for example, grow up with the understanding that people cannot be trusted, that those who say they love them are also apt to hurt them. Is it surprising that such children often become adults who are guarded and wary, who have difficulty in love relationships, and who sometimes abuse their own children? Children who are loved and encouraged, on the other hand, tend to grow up with a happy, trusting outlook; they believe in themselves.

Like the chronology of soil layers revealed in an archaeological dig, your life experiences "stack up" to form your personality. The early years are formative, and each of us begins those years with a certain set of predispositions, the raw materials of personality. These predispositions are not fully understood, but certainly include such things as intellectual capacity and physical attributes. Psychological growth and development continue throughout life as you learn and incorporate new experiences into your view of the world. The process does not suddenly stop at any age. That is, you can and will continue to develop as a person throughout all parts of your life, including in your later life.

You can expect to live and grow throughout your later life in a way that is continuous with your personality. But that doesn't mean that you are locked into an unchangeable pattern. Both older and younger people can change the patterns of personality and coping that do not bring emotional richness and fulfillment. You are never too old to learn and grow.

Some Important Later-Life Mental Health Issues

Medications

Reactions to medications account for up to 25 percent of hospital admissions of older people with mental problems such as confusion, hallucinations, depression, or agitation. Accompanying physical symptoms might include dizziness, sweating, racing pulse, frequent falling, and an unsteady gait. The basic rule of thumb regarding medications is that anything can cause anything. That means prescription, nonprescription, and combinations of medicines. The more pills you take, the more likely you are to have an adverse reaction. Even medications you may have taken for years can suddenly cause you problems, due to changes in the way your body handles them. Always tell each doctor you see about every pill you take. The treatment of medication-related problems is simple—stopping the offending drug. The best cure isn't as good as prevention, however. Have you collected all the pill bottles in your house yet?

Medical Problems

Sometimes older people develop confusion or other mental changes as the first symptom of a physical disorder. When this happens, a person who has been doing well becomes confused, agitated, lethargic, and/or uncommunicative *over a matter of hours to days*. This person may be clearheaded one minute and unable to tell you what year it is the next. In medical terms, the condition is called delirium, and it indicates the need for an aggressive search by a doctor for a physical, reversible cause. It is not "normal" later-life behavior. Causes can include medications, alcohol abuse, metabolic disturbances, infection, cancer, pain, and any number of other physical health problems.

There are other physical changes common in later life that can cause or aggravate mental symptoms. Hearing loss may precipitate paranoia, for example—the idea that others are talking about you or want to harm you. Decreased ability to get around—due to arthritis, for example—can be associated with isolation, loneliness, and boredom, which in turn are associated with depression and further adjustment problems.

Do not assume that any change in your state of mental health is "normal." Talk it over with your doctor. If you have a physical health problem, you don't have to wait until the medical workup is completed to get mental health care. Getting treatment for your emotional problems does not mean you are crazy or weak. It also doesn't mean that you do not have medical problems, that it's "all in your head." When symptoms of both mental and physical problems are present, both should be diagnosed and treated.

Memory Problems

Dementia is the medical word used to refer to long-standing confusion and memory loss. These symptoms develop insidiously, generally over the course of years. Alzheimer's disease is a form of dementia; other causes include long-term drug and alcohol abuse, strokes, and brain injuries. A person with Alzheimer's disease may at first only have trouble with moderately complicated tasks such as using a map. Later, there may be no recollection of recent events, dates, or places. Still later, routine tasks such as using a stove can become dangerous because of the inability to remember and think clearly. By this time the person may need constant supervision. Unfortunately, there is no specific test for Alzheimer's disease, its cause is still a mystery, and there is no cure. As with other chronic diseases of later life, however, adaptation and management for both patient and family are possible, and certainly well worth the effort.

While Alzheimer's disease is popularly equated as a common consequence of old age, only 4–5 percent of the population will get the disease. Another 5–10 percent, however, will develop mild memory disturbance, which persists over the years.[1] Remember, you will not suddenly get Alzheimer's disease, and mild, stable memory trouble is not Alzheimer's disease. Occasional memory lapses are normal and occur in all age groups. If you start having significant memory problems, see your doctor. This is not a "normal" part of later life.

"Normal" Senility

There is no such thing. Period.

Depression

Most people, of all ages, occasionally feel sad or blue. To psychiatrists, however, depression means a pervasively low mood, accompanied by feelings of hopelessness and despair, poor sleep and appetite, low energy, loss of interest or pleasure in sex and other activities, and sometimes thoughts of suicide. Some depressed people get very nervous and upset, worrying excessively about money, death, or physical decline. Others may stop talking altogether, hallucinate, or become convinced that others are trying to hurt or poison them. A seriously depressed person may also have memory and concentration problems similar to those seen in dementia. This "pseudodementia" must be recognized for what it is because it is treatable. It goes away when the depression does.

People get depressed for many reasons. Some kinds of depression can be treated with psychotherapy or medications alone. Others respond best to a combination of psychotherapy and medications. Antidepressant medications do have some side effects, but they are not addictive and they are generally quite safe. Refractory, life-threatening depression is sometimes treated with electroconvulsive therapy. With modern techniques, this procedure is also quite safe and is about like having minor surgery.

If you have symptoms of depression, see a psychiatrist immediately. The condition is treatable, usually with medications and brief psychotherapy, with a success rate of 80–90 percent.

Anxiety

Anxiety is a normal reaction to frightening or upsetting events. Some people, however, develop anxiety disorders, which means that they are nervous, jittery, apprehensive, or fearful, *without* any obvious cause. Physical symptoms often accompany anxiety—sweating, shortness of breath, trembling, heart palpitations, or stomach upset. The anxiety can be persistent and continuous or it can start and stop suddenly, as in a panic attack. Once it is clear that these symptoms are not part of a physical problem, anxiety disorders are treated quite successfully with medications and psychotherapy.

Alcohol Abuse

Yes, that well-coiffed sixty-five-year-old woman in the yellow Cadillac and the kindly seventy-two-year-old grandfather of eight may both be alcoholics. The fifty-five year-old woman who, after her husband's death, starts drinking every night to get to sleep, may end up drinking vodka in her orange juice from morning until night. She will tell no one and no one will suspect for a long time, maybe not until the damage is done. Intoxicated people fall and hit their heads, have car wrecks, and take foolish chances. The risk of suicide is higher in alcoholics, and many are depressed. Alcohol abuse can cause both delirium (in a withdrawal reaction) and dementia (long-term abuse). If it has interfered with your work or relationships, your alcohol use may be a problem, one with devastating mental, physical, and emotional effects. There are many alcohol treatment options, from Alcoholics Anonymous to hospital programs. If you or someone you care about has an alcohol problem, the first step is to ask for help. A good start is to ask a physician for a referral.

Drug Abuse

Drug abuse can become a problem in older people with long-standing pain or anxiety may be present from an earlier age. As with other behaviors and conditions, the recognition of substance abuse is sometimes hampered by the myth that "older people don't do that sort of thing." A doctor is an excellent source for referral to a treatment program.

Adjustment Problems

If you have problems adjusting to later life that are related to life-long conflicts or personality traits, you may benefit from psychotherapy. There are many different kinds, from highly intense forms aimed at helping you discover the roots of long-standing emotional difficulties to brief forms more focused on how to cope in the "here and now." The most important variable in this form of therapy is the relationship you develop with your therapist. Ask your doctor and others for the names of some reputable people if you need this kind of help.

Planning Better Mental Health
in Later Life

Are you clear about the fact that you are more likely to *maintain* your mental health in later life than you are to lose it? If so, let's proceed. Physical, psychological, and social well-being are very much interconnected in later life, and all are important for optimal mental health. Because disturbances in any of these areas will affect your mental health, you are planning for better mental health with every page you read and every worksheet you complete in this book.

The Mental Health Worksheets at the end of this chapter are designed to help you specifically identify potential mental health problems. After you've answered these questions, talk over any concerns you might have with your doctor.

Coping with Mental Health Issues
in Later Life

Part of your personality is how you cope with pain and change. The pain may be mental or physical. Changes may be perceived as good or bad (retirement, for example), but any change requires adjustment. You must adjust to any major life event—retirement, changing jobs, getting married, becoming older, moving, losing a loved one— whether or not you might ordinarily think of it as stressful.

People cope differently according to differences in their personalities. Psychiatrists usually call these ways of coping "defense mechanisms," because they are the ways people defend themselves against mental pain or deal with change. Some of these defense mechanisms work better than others, and some "cost" more than others.

Consider, for example, someone who deals with his frustration about unreasonable work demands by criticizing and yelling at his wife and children. Yes, he vents his anger in a way that doesn't get him fired, but he pays a heavy price in terms of damage to his relationships. The cost of his particular method of coping is high.

One of this man's coworkers does things differently. When he comes home at night, he immediately jogs for an hour in the park near his home. After that he feels ready to interact with the important people in his life, without a lot of "static" from his job frustrations. His defense mechanism works, and he gets physically fit in the process.

Different people have different ways of coping, and some work better than others. However, any coping mechanism can be overwhelmed under difficult circumstances. What then? If you are unable to cope with what goes on in your life, you will develop mental symptoms such as anxiety, depression, irritability, or confused thinking. You may develop physical symptoms. You may feel (or people may tell you) that your basic personality has changed. Not so. Your coping mechanisms have been overwhelmed.

There is nothing mysterious about any of this, in spite of the fact that there is much we do not know. Being overwhelmed is not irreversible. The important thing for you to know is that if you do develop mental symptoms, you can get help in analyzing what happened to overwhelm you, and you can learn better ways of coping. Don't let our society's stigma and ignorance about mental symptoms prevent you from getting help if you need it.

What Is Normal and What Is Not

Is it normal to be mentally healthy in later life? For a person your age? A person your age plus ten years? Plus twenty years? Did you change your ideas about what was normal when you thought of people older than yourself? If so, think again. Only about 1–2 percent of the population has a first psychiatric hospitalization in later life.[2] Just as you shouldn't fear becoming physically ill or disabled as soon as you retire, or when you reach some arbitrary "old age," you also shouldn't fear becoming crazy, senile, boring, or unhappy.

Mental decline is not inevitable in later life. Self-esteem, active involvement with the world and the people around you, straight thinking, honest feelings, and the capacity to cope with whatever troubles come your way are the normal characteristics of a healthy person of any age. But norms and standards of life at one stage are not always appropriate for other stages. You don't apply the same measurement to a two-year-old as to an adolescent, and you don't expect the adolescent to behave as an adult. Does it make any sense to assume that later life is "supposed" to be just like earlier life?

The answer to that question is an emphatic **no!** In the words of Carl Jung:

> A human being would certainly not grow to be seventy or eighty years old if this longevity had no meaning for the species to which he belongs. The afternoon of life must also have a significance of its own and cannot merely be a pitiful appendage to life's morning. . . . Whoever carries over into the afternoon the law of the morning . . . must pay for so doing with damage to his soul.

The infant wants to be fed and changed and held, the toddler to explore new worlds but run back to Mom in case of danger. The schoolchild reaches outside the family and tries new things independently. The adolescent struggles for individual identity and sometimes rejects the parents. The young adult prepares for career and family. You consolidated your career and raised your children in earlier adulthood. What is your developmental task in later life?

The developmental tasks of later life involve going beyond the rigid, sharply defined roles of early life. Instead, perhaps you can think of it as a culmination of development, a time when fixed roles are no longer necessary[3] and greater individual variation is a sign of achievement. *In later life you can more easily be the person you want to be.*

Keep in mind that "different" is not the same thing as "abnormal." Consider crying, for example. Some people cry at the beauty of a sunset or the poignant triumph of a child's first steps. Some people cry when they are nervous or mad, others at times of sorrow. Some people cry only when they're chopping onions! Does that mean that people who don't cry don't hurt inside? Or that people who do cry are weak and silly? Of course not. It only means that people express themselves in many different ways. Priorities are different and personalities are different. Ways of coping are different.

A mentally healthy person can think straight and relate to others in a meaningful way, is curious and involved in life, and has an overall sense of well-being. This person can solve problems when they occur and is flexible enough to adjust in the face of adversity. In later life, mentally healthy people bring the coping strategies of a lifetime to bear successfully on whatever changes come with age or retirement.

The Head Bone's Connected
to the Rest of the Body

Many different things can affect your mental health in later life. At no time in your life will the lines between physical, psychological, and social factors blur more than in the later years. Just think for a minute. Suppose you find your income decreased by half—a common social factor for retired people. Now suppose that you have high blood pressure and arthritis, and that you take two different medications for each of these problems. In addition, one of your children is going through an acrimonious divorce, and you are trying to help take care of your grandchildren. You begin to have trouble sleeping and don't feel much like eating. You lose twenty pounds and feel tired all the time, without your usual interest in things. Your arthritis pain bothers you more and you start losing track of your medicines. Did you take two pills this morning or one? Maybe you didn't take any at first and later took three to catch up. You start to see little point in getting out of bed each day, and become convinced that you have some terrible disease. However, the situation seems so hopeless that you can see no reason to try to find out.

What is wrong with you? Your weight loss could be due to depression, cancer, pain, or lack of money for food. Your confusion could be caused by depression, lack of sleep, pain, or an inadvertent overdose of pain pills. Your depression could be related to the stress in your family. You may not be coping as well as you have in the past because of your confusion, fatigue, or depression. Depression is also linked to physical illness, some kinds of high blood pressure medication, and social isolation. Maybe you are trying to save money by taking pills prescribed for someone else, and you are slowly developing serious side effects.

Do you see how all of these things are connected? If you have ever had a headache when you faced a difficult day at work, you are well aware that physical and mental symptoms commonly occur together. You also know that having a fight with your spouse is unlikely to make your head feel any better.

These are everyday events. Unfortunately, however, because of the stigma attached to the concept of mental illness, people in our society often fail to realize the importance of dealing with the emotional aspects of human suffering, as well as with the physical. Taking an aspirin for your headache, for example, may make the pain go away for a time. But it doesn't help you cope with your problem at work, or improve your relationships with important people in your life.

The state of your physical and mental health, the strength of your relationships, what you do with your time, and how much money you have are all interwoven in later life. And when mental health problems arise in later life, they are often associated with physical problems and/or difficulty adjusting to changing life circumstances. Each of these events is connected to all of the others, and it is the combination to which you must adjust.

Rosemary Krale is a good example. At age seventy-six, she and her husband of fifty-five years lived in a home that they had owned outright for some years. Arthur Krale was physically debilitated from a stroke and Mrs. Krale spent much of her time caring for him. She also had a number of successful, active children and grandchildren whom she saw frequently. Her own health was quite good. She felt fit and well most days and was mentally sharp, besting many a younger person with her up-to-the-minute knowledge of current world affairs.

On a sunny Tuesday morning while driving her husband to a doctor's appointment, their car was hit at high speed on a freeway entrance ramp. Mr. Krale was unharmed, but Mrs. Krale was hospitalized with a very painful broken shoulder. On her third day in the hospital, psychiatrists were asked to see Mrs. Krale because she was confused, not sleeping at night, seeing things, and accusing her nurses of trying to poison her.

Mrs. Krale was not suddenly senile. She was reacting with mental symptoms to her physical pain, the pain medications she was taking, the unaccustomed environment of the hospital, her worry about her husband, and the anxiety associated with the accident itself. With a change in her medication, decreased pain, and increased ability to move around again, Mrs. Krale was back to normal by the time she left the hospital a couple of weeks later.

You can look at this same situation from Mr. Krale's point of view. Suppose Mrs. Krale had been unable to return home for a longer time. He would then have had to cope with not having her there, as well as with his own physical problems. Financial strain would have increased because someone would have to be hired to take care of him. Perhaps a nursing home would have been the only alternative. That would have separated the couple and destroyed their financial security, and would have required a devastating emotional adjustment for each of them.

In later life, serious physical, psychological, or social problems rarely occur as separate and unrelated events. Much more often such problems are found together, and trying to deal with one isolated area is not only futile, it's dangerous. The body and the mind work together. Each affects the other, and both influence and are influenced by whatever life circumstances are present. In other words, the head bone *is* connected to the rest of the body.

Getting Help if You Need It

The first step in planning for good mental health is to recognize when to get help. The second is to be willing to get it, and the third is to know how to get it.

Overall, mental health problems are at least as common in older people as in younger, and adults over sixty-five constitute more than 10 percent of the population. Yet, older people make up only 4 percent of the population at mental health clinics, and get only 1 percent of the treatment time.[4] In contrast, the average internist spends 40 percent of his or her time with older people. Many people who could use thorough psychiatric evaluation and treatment in their later years are not getting it.

Why are older people not getting their fair share of the mental health care in this country? The reasons involve the history of the mental health care system, the caregivers, and older people themselves.

The first major form of mental health treatment was psychoanalysis, developed by Sigmund Freud. Psychoanalysis is an intensive form of psychotherapy, aimed at discovering the basic roots of the thoughts, feelings, and behavior patterns that are causing the patient's difficulties. This form of treatment was originally not felt to be appropriate for older people because of its length (as many as four or five sessions a week for several years), intensity, and expense, as well as because older people were not thought able to change enough to benefit significantly in their lifetimes. (You know better than that now, right?) This attitude has been modified in recent years, but probably has continued to influence the mental health care system.

Some mental health care personnel may avoid working with older people because it is hard to listen to someone talk about what it's like to grow old or to face illness and death. Such topics are reminders of one's own mortality and make many people anxious. Psychotherapists are no exception, though more and more are becoming aware of the need to educate themselves further in this area.

Expense is another problem in getting adequate mental health care, and insurance coverage for mental health care—including that provided by Medicare and Medicaid—has long been inadequate. These inequities reflect society's bias in favor of physical explanations for health problems, with most policies providing almost limitless coverage for physical problems, compared with absurdly limited psychiatric coverage. Some older people see general practice doctors for their psychiatric problems because they can't afford to see the specialist in psychiatry. In some cases this results in inadequate or even ineffective care. Therefore the problem continues and worsens, with adverse effects on the quality, and sometimes length, of the older person's life. Such neglect is very costly in both money and human misery.

Would you be willing to look for help if you needed it? The reluctance of many older people to ask for help when they are in emotional pain may be the most difficult barrier to overcome. This attitude is understandable in a society that veils mental illness and its treatment in cloaks of mystery and stigma. Don't be a hero. If you are having problems, get help immediately. Being able to do this is a sign of good judgment and of *good mental health*!

Suppose the loss of a loved one has produced a profound grief, now shading into depression. Or you are having trouble adjusting to some other major life change, in spite of all your best efforts. How do you decide where to go for help? Because of the relationship between physical health problems and mental health, as a general rule you should see your doctor first. Be frank about your symptoms, including the emotional ones.

Roberta Lyons went to see her doctor the day before she killed herself. She told him about her arthritis pain and her stomachaches, her back trouble, and her angina. What she didn't tell him was that she was so depressed she could barely get out of bed in the morning. She reviewed her will, carefully refilled her medication prescriptions, then went home that afternoon and took them all with a bottle of gin.

It's sad when physical illness disrupts a life. It's tragic when treatable depression kills. Telling your doctor how you feel emotionally can be the first step to getting help.

How to Find Help for Mental Health Problems

Mental health care is provided by an array of people trained to different levels in different fields. There are psychiatrists, psychologists, social workers, nurses, nurse practitioners, counselors, educators, clergy, and a host of other people who offer therapies based on everything from diet and exercise to regular enemas.

To make matters even more confusing, there are different kinds of treatments offered by even the most conventional mental health care providers. These forms of therapy include medications, individual psychotherapy of many different varieties, group psychotherapy, family therapy, marital therapy, self-help groups, education-based counseling, crisis intervention—the list can be expanded almost to infinity. Some mental health care is administered in hospitals, some in clinics, and some in private offices.

For most older people, especially if you have not had emotional problems before, or you are not really sure what the problem is, medical background is important. *You should first see someone who is trained to recognize psychological symptoms that could be coming from physical causes.* That usually means a medical doctor, either your own primary care doctor or a psychiatrist.

A psychiatrist is a medical doctor who has received additional training in the diagnosis and treatment of mental disorders. Some psychiatrists, like some internists, have received even further training in the care of older people (geriatrics). Psychiatrists, as medical doctors, can prescribe medications and take care of people in the hospital as well as in their offices. Some forms of depression and other mental disorders are best treated with the use of medications, and it can be dangerous to delay these medications if they are needed. Psychiatrists also provide individual, group, and family therapy.

How do you find a good psychiatrist? Your doctor knows your medical community. He or she can provide you with the names of some reputable people. You also can obtain names from friends who have been in treatment, from the local medical society, or from your area agency on aging (in the phone book—often under city/county listings). If there is a medical school in your town, you may be able to use one of their clinics, and community mental health centers are another resource.

If you and your doctor are convinced that the physical causes or contributors to your emotional problem have been or are being adequately investigated, and *if* there is no indication for medications, you may then wish to seek help from mental health care providers who are not medical doctors. This group includes psychologists, social workers, nurses, and counselors. Care from nonmedical therapists may be less expensive; you can get names from the same resources listed above.

Finally, there are a number of self-help groups available now. Many are offered at low or no fee, and you may want to use them in addition to professional help. It can be very comforting to know there are other people out there who are having some of the same problems as you, and you can share ideas. For example, there are now a number of self-help groups for families of patients with Alzheimer's disease.

Caution: Stick with reputable, permanently based, well-established groups and therapists. Beware of any that are very expensive, promise things that seem too good to be true, or employ questionable methods. Some states do not have strict licensing requirements, and anyone can set up shop as a therapist or counselor. Try to get some kind of reference if you are not sure. No one wants to spend money on quackery!

Any mental health or adjustment problems you had when younger are likely to follow you into your later years, and unexpected financial, physical, or social hardship may "unmask" problems that were well compensated before. But remember that it is not natural or normal to be depressed, confused, or unhappy in later life. Neither aging nor retirement are universally bad: Your life may change, but it still can be satisfying. You should be able to adjust. If you can't, get professional help. Deal with your losses, whatever they are.

Good adjustment to later life is basically a mental process, and in that sense better mental health is the essential focus of all your work in this book. Getting accurate information and making plans will improve your self-esteem and your sense of control. You can see yourself as a unique and important person with options in life.

Retirement, growing older, the prospect of illness or your own death, illness and deaths among friends and family, changes in social status and financial well-being all require adaptation. That most older people do adjust adequately is indeed a testament to their strength, resiliency, and coping abilities. In fact, a third of people over sixty-five describe their "retirement period" as the best years of their lives.[5] There's a good chance you can, too!

Things to Think About

1. Mental decline is not "normal" in later life.
2. You deserve the most satisfying later life you can get, whatever that may mean to you.
3. You are never too old to learn and to grow.
4. Your head bone's connected to the rest of your body: Physical, psychological, and social factors all are important for mental health in later life.
5. Having a mental health problem does not mean you are weak or crazy.
6. In your later life you *can* receive and benefit from mental health care: It's the smart thing to do.

Notes

1. L. S. Libow, "Health care during the retirement years," in *Aging and Retirement: Prospects, Planning, and Policy*, eds. N. G. McCluskey and E. P. Borgatta (Beverly Hills and London: Sage Publications, 1981).

2. R A. Kalish, "Human behavior and aging: An overview," in *The Later Years: Social Applications of Gerontology* (Monterey, Calif.: Brooks/Cole Publishing Co., 1977).

3. A. Weinberger, "Psychological well being in retirement," ibid.

4. See note 1 above.

5. See note 1 above.

MENTAL HEALTH WORKSHEET 8.1
Physical Factors

1. Are you taking the medications you need to take for your physical problems?

2. Are you taking any you don't need to take? (For example, if your doctor says that you won't need the high blood pressure pills if you cut out the salt and lose fifty pounds, then get busy: Cut out the salt and lose fifty pounds!)

3. Do you know the names and doses of all the medicines you take? Do you have the list with you? Have you gone over it with each of your doctors? Have you updated any changes?

4. Do you smoke? Do you drink more than one or two alcoholic drinks per day? Do you take any unprescribed drugs?

5. Have you had any legal or relationship problems connected with your use of alcohol or drugs?

6. Do you have a doctor who has time to talk to you—one who knows or is willing to learn about some of the particular problems of older people? One who understands the importance of mental as well as physical health and says so?

7. Do you have any new physical symptoms or recent changes in your usual state of physical or mental health? Have you seen your doctor about them?

8. Do you realize the importance of getting help for both physical *and* mental problems if you have symptoms of either or both?

MENTAL HEALTH WORKSHEET 8.2
Mental Factors

1. Do you have enough mental challenge in your life? If not, what can you do now to begin a "mental aerobics" program? (See chapters 5 and 6 for some ideas.)

2. Will retirement change your level of intellectual and emotional stimulation? What can you do now to prepare for these changes?

3. Do you generally feel good about yourself and your life? If not, why not? What can you do now to make some changes?

4. Is your mood generally stable and optimistic?

5. Do you sleep and eat well? Have you lost weight recently without going on a diet?

6. Can you concentrate and enjoy things as well as you used to?

7. Have you noticed any changes in your sexual interest? Is your sex life satisfactory?

8. Do you have plenty of energy and motivation to do things?

9. Have you recently thought about suicide or found yourself preoccupied with death?

10. Have you had memory problems or uncharacteristic emotional outbursts?

11. Are you nervous or jittery much of the time without knowing why?

12. Do you feel that you are coping well with any changes in your life? If not, why? Have you sought professional help?

MENTAL HEALTH WORKSHEET 8.3
Social Factors

1. Are your relationships with other people satisfactory? Why or why not? What can you do to change things now? (See chapter 9.)

2. Does your life seem balanced between stability and challenge? between time with others and time alone? between work and play? If not, have you started making changes? (See chapters 5 and 6.)

3. Are you dealing reasonably well with any losses you've experienced?

4. Are your finances in order? (See chapter 10.)

5. Have you thoroughly explored the question of whether or not to retire? Do you know what kind of later life you want and how you are going to get it? (See chapters 5 and 6.)

6. Do you understand that you are an important and worthwhile person, regardless of your age and work status? Do you know what to expect as you get older, and do you feel that you are going to be able to cope and adjust?

If your honest answers to any of these questions raise any concerns, don't be afraid to seek help.

9 Relationships

For two human beings who are dependent on one another to live at peace is the rarest and most difficult of ethical and intellectual accomplishments.

—Herman Hesse

What to Know about
Relationships in Later Life

A relationship is nothing more than the state of being connected in some way. The critical factor in human relationships is the feeling of being connected to another person, which is a basic need for most people, although different people need different degrees and types of contact with others. You can think about your relationships in three basic categories: romantic or sexual, blood relations, and friends. For convenience, I will often refer to the significant other people in your life as partners or spouses, but the same principles apply no matter what the relationship. To whatever extent you are sharing this time of life with another person, you need to plan it together, especially if there is any merger of finances, living arrangements, or other interdependence. You and your friends and family may have some later-life adjustments to make, the magnitude of which depends on how much your lifestyle and roles change. It's especially important to learn to keep sight of your own objectives and needs, while maintaining an appropriate level of concern and flexibility toward those of the other person.

What do you get from relationships with other people? The particulars vary from person to person, but healthy love relationships and friendships provide a sense of self-worth, sharing and togetherness, and feelings of belonging to part of a larger whole and of helping and being helped. Closeness and caring can give balance and perspective

122

to life. Lonely Russian novelist Turgenev cried, "I would give up all my fame and all my art if there were one woman who cared whether or not I came home late to dinner."

An earlier theory of aging, called the disengagement theory, held that older people and society slowly withdraw from one another. The psychological well-being that comes from this process was thought to be universal. It turns out, however, that older people aren't really all that different from other people; social interaction remains part of maintaining a healthy sense of well-being.[1] If right now you are angry, laughing, or shaking your head in amazement at the thought of yourself losing your need for other people in your later years, or of that loss being considered a sign of psychological health when a person is older, good for you! That means you are beginning to recognize the myths of ageism for what they are, and to trust your own reactions to them.

Today, more older people do live alone or with unrelated other people than in the past, but this is largely because high incomes allow for this (preferred) living arrangement. Fewer than 10 percent of people over sixty-five report feeling lonely, without friends or isolated from family, although younger people tend to believe that such feelings are almost universally present among older people.[2]

Loving and sharing your life with other people, then, does not become any less important in later life. Think about the people in your life now—friends, lovers, partners, neighbors, children, grandchildren. How often do you see these people? How well do you really know them? When was the last time you told them how much you care? Communication and consideration are the watchwords for success in relationships, no matter how long you've been together.

Consider an example: Wallace and Esther Ida owned the home they had lived in for forty-five years. Their neighborhood, like their marriage, was comfortable and stable. They had been friends for twenty years with another couple somewhat more financially well off, and after retirement the four decided to move into a retirement community in a warmer climate, far away from their hometown. Too late, the Idas realized that there were a number of hidden costs in the purchase contract for their home in the retirement community, costs that they could ill afford. Their activities were curtailed by their budget, and they could not do many of the things their old friends were doing. The situation was further complicated by the fact that Mr. and Mrs. Ida found that they disliked living in "the compound," as they came to call it, partly because they preferred to be around people of all ages.

Moving back to the old neighborhood was out of the question because inflation had driven housing costs beyond their means.

Wallace and Esther Ida were lucky because their marriage was strong enough to weather these storms. They managed, with humor, love, and kindness (and occasional arguments) to avoid blaming and retreating from each other in ways that could have dealt enduring damage to their relationship. You can learn something from their troubles and from their example. The important things to know about relationships can be summarized as follows:

1. People need relationships.
2. Relationships need continual nurturing.
3. Nurturing relationships requires consideration.
4. Nurturing relationships requires communication.
5. Communication must include certain specifics.

People Need Relationships

Human beings are herd animals. We were not designed to go through life entirely alone. You need someone to love, to listen to you, to talk with, laugh with, fight with, and make love with; someone to rub your back when it hurts; someone to appreciate you when you return the favor; someone to work with, play with, compete with, and share with. Romance and passion, the love of a child, the concern of a parent, the quiet comfort of an old friend—none of these exist without other people. Age is not the issue. At the age of forty or sixty or ninety you do not "outgrow" your need for satisfying relationships.

Relationships Need Nurturing

As surely as relationships do not exist in a vacuum, they also do not grow and thrive of their own accord. Trite but true: You have to work at it.

Nurturing Relationships
Requires Consideration

When Mr. and Mrs. Ida first found out about some of the hidden costs in their contract with the retirement community, each was tempted to blame the other for not having been astute enough to foresee the problem. They also felt misled by their longtime friends, who had encouraged them and who had made many of the initial arrangements. Several weeks of repeatedly heated discussions usually began with one partner wondering why the other had not asked "*his* friends" or "*her* friends" about some detail in the contract, and culminated in angry recriminations, hurt silence, and slammed doors. Days would pass in uneasy truce until another "innocent" remark triggered the cycle again. Soon, however, they realized the futility of these attempts to place blame, and they set up some ground rules for their talks. They posted an index card on the refrigerator door that read simply "50–50" to remind them that they both had agreed to the move. Whenever the blaming started, one of them would simply point to the card—their signal to stop the conversation until they could refocus on solving the problem at hand, rather than on hurtful remarks and defensive arguments. In other words, they enforced kindness and consideration in order to nurture their relationship through a difficult time.

You must be considerate of your partner's thoughts and feelings as well as of your own. This balance can be tricky to achieve, especially when emotions run high; however, the payoff is great. Esther and Wallace Ida could not (and were right not to) cover up their strong feelings. But they also could not work together to solve their problems until they agreed they had entered into the contract as partners, and that they wanted to find the solutions the same way. Being able to agree in this way and make the extra effort to understand each other allowed them to be considerate in spite of their strong feelings.

Ask yourself if you usually accord your partner the same respect, understanding, and consideration you would give a friend or acquaintance. Familiarity can breed contempt (which is all the more devastating, since the better you know another person, the better you can aim for his or her weak spots), but it doesn't have to. To nurture your relationships, let familiarity breed respect and consideration instead.

Nurturing Relationships
Requires Communication

Couples in therapy often are surprised to discover, when they are asked to keep track of it, how little they really communicate. One busy couple calculated that, in the course of a week, they spent about two hours and fifteen minutes talking to each other about something other than their schedules, who was going to pick up the kids or take them to piano lessons, grocery shopping, phone messages, and household chores. Almost none of that two hours and and fifteen minutes was spent talking about the relationship itself or about each person's part in it.

Time spent really talking and really listening to each other is time invested in the relationship. What does "really talking and really listening" mean? It means sitting down together with the goal of communicating with each other. It means turning off the television, closing the book, and concentrating on the other person. How? Really listen to what your partner is telling you, ask questions, answer questions, tell the joke you heard at work, explain how you felt deep down inside when your brother made that hurtful remark at dinner last week. Talk about the relationship itself: Is it working? Did you appreciate something your partner did for you recently? Are there hurt or angry feelings you haven't discussed? The goal of communication is to understand the other person, and to get the other person to understand you.

Good communication is essential for people who are planning to spend their later lives together. Think of it as relationship maintenance. Cars break down if you don't maintain them, and so do relationships. Know each other's expectations and concerns about getting older, about retirement, and about any life changes you expect to make. You can share ideas and ways to solve problems. You might even discover some new and exciting things about that person you married forty years ago! You've changed, haven't you? You're an interesting person, aren't you? Don't forget that your partner is, too. The couple I mentioned above started making "communication appointments" with each other for half an hour each weekday and an hour on the weekends. They regularly "ran overtime" and rediscovered each other in the process.

Communication Must Include
Certain Specifics

To nurture your friendships, you must talk to each other. To plan later life together, you must be sure that your talk eventually covers certain key items. These items include how and to what extent you will take care of each other if there is serious physical or mental illness, how to manage financially in the event of death or illness of your partner, how you want to spend your time and money, where to live, what effect retirement will have on either or both partners, and management of grief over the inevitable losses. Legal matters, especially property transfer, are critically important, and *both* partners must be well versed in the day-to-day management of family, financial, and social responsibilities.

Use and develop your communication skills and plan together. Each of you must understand the other's desires, dreams, and expectations for later life. For example, have you made the assumption that your partner wants to retire at the same time and in the same way as you do? Do you have in the back of your mind that you and your spouse will be spending a lot more time together after retirement? What if your partner doesn't share that idea? Such things are best talked about explicitly. Don't get your mental bags packed for Hawaii only to find that your partner has office space rented for his or her new consulting business. And check with your kids before moving three thousand miles just to be closer to them! Would you still want to be there if they were transferred elsewhere?

Partners, families, and friends who do not carefully and thoroughly discuss later-life plans may find themselves swept into the midst of turmoil, just at the time when they had envisioned enjoying increased time together.

Planning Better Relationships in Later Life

Building and maintaining strong and satisfying later-life relationships depends on communication and consideration. Each partner wants to get her or his own needs met, but not at the expense of the relationship. You and your partner have to understand one another and be able to compromise, to both talk and listen, to allow the time and energy to maintain honesty and a commitment to the relationship. Be at least as polite to each other as you are to casual acquaintances—this alone will prevent or solve a lot of problems.

These principles of effective communication are the same across all the life phases, but in later life you must think and plan more carefully to nurture your relationships. This chapter will help you.

First you will assess and clarify your own thoughts, feelings, and expectations. Then you will share them with your partner during uninterrupted time you have scheduled together. Some issues will be more difficult to resolve or talk about than others. That's okay. If you need more time, take it. If the process becomes too confused or heated, stop and start over later. Keep trying until it works.

If your marriage (or whatever relationship you're working on) is in good shape, and you already communicate well with each other, these principles will guide you relatively quickly through some of the common problem areas. If you have trouble communicating with each other, you can expect to take more time with each issue. Think of it as acquiring a new skill. It's no different from other skills. Some of you, for example, will be more adept at managing your finances than your relationships. That doesn't mean you can't do it, only that you have to work at it more. The communication process is what counts.

Sometimes people are afraid to talk to each other about how they really feel, especially if there is conflict. You may worry that you or your partner will cry or get mad or both. There is nothing wrong with that. The expression of strong feelings can be good and useful. It indicates that you are dealing with important things. But conflicts and strong emotional expressions can scare people into silence in our "chin up and keep it all under control" society. We may feel guilty or frustrated or afraid, and then lose track of or hold back what we really want to say because of these reactions. How can you keep this from happening?

One way to ensure that communication continues, even in the face of conflict or strong feelings, is to establish some ground rules for your talks. The "rules" that follow are examples. You may want to add a few of your own, as dictated by your particular needs.

Ground Rules for Good Communication

1. Speak for yourself. One of the quickest ways to start a fight that stops communication is to begin any sentence with "You always (or never) . . ." Most people don't like to be rigidly categorized. Even if what you say is true, the chance of getting the rest of your message across is very low. Try starting your sentences with "I." Rephrasing things this way serves two purposes. First, it is less likely to evoke a knee-jerk negative response from your partner. Second, changing the wording of a tired old complaint may allow you to realize that there really is another issue at stake. "You're always on the phone or watching television" may be what you say, for example, when what you really mean is "I'm lonely and I'd like to talk to you."

2. No hitting. Two people cannot communicate openly if one is afraid of being hurt by the other. That's obvious with regard to physical injury. But words can be used as weapons just like fists. The bruises and scars don't show but they are there. Hitting, whether physical or verbal, stops communication.

3. Respect emotions. Emotional expressiveness is part of what makes us humans different from the average houseplant. Your feelings are part of you—love, anger, sadness, joy. There is no "wrong" feeling,

though admittedly some feelings are more fun than others. Don't try to cover up strong feelings. (It won't work anyway.) And don't put your partner down for showing strong feelings. (You won't accomplish anything.) Trusting another person with how you really feel can be scary at first, but it's an important form of communication.

4. Minimize blaming. Remember the couple who posted their 50–50 blame distribution on the refrigerator door? They saved themselves a lot of time and hurt feelings by not allowing the "who's to blame" question to keep creeping into (and ruining) their discussions and their problem solving. If you and your partner are prone to spend a lot of time passing the blame back and forth, look for ways to stop. Suppose, for example, that your partner has never let you forget that time you lost $3,000 (and two years' vacations) on an ill-considered stock purchase. You can't seem to talk about your financial plans without returning to that twenty-year-old argument. Give it up. Admit your mistake, ask your partner what you can do to atone, and agree to forget the incident. Then get on with life, without all the interference!

5. Retire the old stuff. There may be another reason for your partner's continual reminders about the stock loss. Sometimes old arguments hang on because the underlying problem is still there. Maybe your partner keeps bringing up the stock loss because he or she felt and still feels excluded from the decision-making process in your relationship. Carefully examine any recurring arguments, ones that don't seem to get resolved long after their time is past. Ask yourselves whether there is some bigger hurt or misunderstanding to be reconciled. Talk about it and look for ways to resolve it. This is one time when retirement definitely is in order!

6. Make it fun. Making plans for your later life together need not be a chore. Take your time and set it up as a pleasant experience. Make a date with each other. Go out for dinner. Relax with a glass of wine and some soft music. Try to avoid talking about sensitive issues when one of you is already tired or upset. Take breaks for remembering good times together.

7. Remember your manners. There's still a lot to be said for good, old-fashioned politeness. Saying please and thank you, remembering birthdays and anniversaries, and expressing love and appreciation work as well in the later phases of a relationship as in the beginning. Surprise her with flowers. Take him a special book. The expression is simple but effective.

Now that you have a few guiding principles, it's time to start putting them into practice. In the first exercise, you will assess the current status of your relationship. No two relationships are exactly the same. The better you can characterize what has and has not worked for you in the past, the better you can plan for the challenges ahead of you. You will probably be spending more time together in later life. You may be adjusting to retirement or other lifestyle changes. Your body may feel or function differently. Your goal is to develop a productive way of thinking and talking about the changes; there are no magic answers.

The Relationship Worksheets at the end of this chapter give you a format for talking about some of the more common changes. First, answer the questions without discussing them with your partner. Then set aside time together to talk about your ideas, feelings, and possible actions. Answer the questions as honestly and openly as possible. If you "cheat" by writing down what you think you *should* feel, the power of the exercises as tools for nurturing your later relationships will be greatly diminished. Remember that the worksheets are just that—tools. The goal is to *communicate, considerately.*

Coping with Relationship Issues
in Later Life

The picture Mrs. Johnson held in her hand was torn and creased, and at first it was hard to realize that it had been taken only four years earlier. Mr. and Mrs. Johnson had been photographed on their way to one of their many social functions: he, elegant in his black tuxedo, she in her deep blue ball gown, linked arm in arm with her lover of forty-two years. Mr. Johnson had died suddenly of a heart attack two years afterward, and Mrs. Johnson sobbed as she told me how much she missed him. They had lived a fairy-tale life, she said, marred only by the fact that they had never been able to have children. They had kept such a special spark between them that people always thought they were newlyweds.

For the first year after Mr. Johnson died, Mrs. Johnson tried hard to keep busy. But as each birthday or anniversary came and went, she became more and more depressed. No other man could ever replace what she had with her beloved husband, and she told friends she sometimes wished she had died with him.

Mrs. Johnson was depressed. She responded only partially to treatment with medications. The other part of her treatment involved helping her come to terms with the loss of the most important person in her life. As hard as it is to think about, you are more likely to lose a loved one in later life than at any other time in your life. This is a major stress. My grandmother, using her dry wit to cope with the number of deaths and illnesses of longtime friends in her small and close-knit rural community, once wondered aloud if there could be something in the water.

You can lose friends through death, divorce, or when they (or you) move away. You can lose contacts with people after retirement. Your spouse could be stricken with an illness that renders him or her unable to communicate or interact with you meaningfully—a loss that is sometimes even harder to deal with than death. These things happen. But if both of you think about them together now, your plans can be a source of great comfort during the turbulent emotions that follow a major loss.

Grief is a normal psychological response to the loss of someone who has been important to you. Studies have shown that most people experience particular kinds of feelings in a fairly similar sequence after a loss. Of course, as you recall, different people react differently to similar events. These stages of grief are not rigid or strictly defined, but they represent the major elements in a gradual progression of adjustment.

First, there is **disbelief**. You just can't believe that your loved one is gone. It's impossible. You just talked to him or her last week or yesterday. Then there is **anger**—at the illness, at fate, at God, at the doctor, even at the loved one who has left you. As the feelings of **sadness** break through, they are very intense at first and are only gradually interspersed with less intense periods of increasing length. Anger and sadness are part of the normal and necessary grief process, and nothing is served by trying not to feel these things, or by feeling guilty about them. But it helps to know that the pain doesn't last forever.

Finally, the distress gives way to a progressive **acceptance** of the loss. You can move on with life in a new way, carrying your memories of your loved one with you.

Sometimes people have trouble grieving their losses and going on with their lives. This may be because of long-standing personality traits that make it harder to cope with loss or change. Or because there are too many other things happening at once. In the space of a single year, Martha Alden retired from the office where she had worked for seven-

teen years, moved from San Francisco back to Seattle, developed serious heart problems, and lost her husband. Understandably, it was very
hard for her to deal with all of these changes at one time, and she became seriously depressed, in spite of her previously well-adjusted life.

Lois Rosen found that, even though she and her husband argued
continually through twenty-five years of marriage, she completely fell
apart after he was gone. Albert Rosen had been unfaithful to Lois
many times, and they were never really able to communicate. She
complained bitterly about his emotional coldness, and had often
thought of leaving him. She told herself and her friends that she
stayed with him because he was a good provider in spite of his other
shortcomings. Furthermore, she was aware that she herself had a pattern of getting involved in self-destructive relationships. When her
husband suddenly died after a stroke, Lois Rosen collapsed emotionally. She began to drink too much and continually felt guilty for "not
having been a better wife."

Surprisingly, it's sometimes harder to cope with the loss of someone
with whom you've had a difficult relationship. There can be many reasons for this—feeling guilty about having wished the person gone
during arguments in the past, being unable to come to terms with re-
membered hurts, believing that it is "not right" to be angry anymore—
as many reasons as there are people to devise them. If you find yourself in this kind of situation, you may need professional help to work
out your problems.

Another thing to think about if you lose your spouse is how you
will meet your emotional need for closeness. Do you want a new partner? Will your friends and family be enough? How will you meet your
sexual needs? These are serious matters, and there is nothing wrong or
bad about considering what you might do. Certainly, while you are
still grieving your loss, you probably won't be thinking in these terms.
But later, continuing to feel lonely without doing anything about it is
not the way to get the most out of your life. Dating, being sexually active, or marrying again are not equivalent to being immoral or unfaithful to the memory of your partner who is gone.

Because of life span differences, older women far outnumber older
men, and meeting people can be a problem. Some people join clubs or
take classes. Others go dancing regularly at places that cater to older
people. Some older couples even find it comforting to talk with each
other about this issue.

Coming to emotional terms with the loss of a significant person in your life is only part of your task. Think specifically about how the loss of your spouse would affect you financially and socially. Would you still want to live in the same place? Keep the same activities? See the same friends? How much income would you lose? How would your budget change? What if one of you becomes physically or mentally unable to care for himself or herself? Talking about these matters *before they become problems* is essential. By talking through the possibilities in advance, you'll learn something about each other and your relationship, and you'll be able to make better plans in all areas. If you discover, for example, that your spouse knows full well that that he or she does not want to ever live in that retirement community without you, the two of you may decide to reconsider moving there at all.

Getting Help if You Need It

At the most extreme, serious medical or psychiatric illness can impair thought processes or physical abilities to the point that people can no longer care for themselves or make decisions. This is a tremendously painful process for everyone involved, but you should know that there are ways to legally change responsibility for financial and other decisions from one individual to another. This is usually called legal guardianship and setting it up can be quite complicated. You will need a lawyer to help you.

What do you do if your relationships don't seem to be working? For example:

You and your husband can't seem to get through to each other anymore, or every time you try to sit down for a planning session, old disagreements interfere.

Your wife is exhausted to the point of physical illness, mainly from the strain of caring for her invalid father. He's had a stroke and can no longer recognize her or care for himself, but she can't face the idea of a nursing home.

One of your children is having serious marital problems. You're trying to help, but your own life feels as if it's slipping away.

You lost your spouse last year but haven't been able to get past the grief and go on with your life. You can't seem to shake the sadness, you hate to "burden" others by continuing to talk about your loss, so you've stopped going out at all. You may be depressed.

What kind of help should you seek? As you can surmise from the variety of life situations described above, that depends on the problem. How to find the right help for emotional problems was discussed in the chapter on mental health. Remember that grief is not the same thing as depression. If you are not feeling as if you are at least on the road to recovery within a few weeks of a major loss, seek a professional consultation. By "on the road to recovery," I do not mean that you are feeling good again, but you should at least be able to eat and sleep more normally. You should not be continuously depressed, isolated, or crying uncontrollably. Most people wait too long to get help. Better sooner than later.

For difficulties within your relationships, marital or otherwise, family therapy may be helpful. The therapist can help you look at problems together, identify sources of trouble in the relationship, learn better communication skills, and generate new ways of looking at old conflicts. You can turn a troubled time into a new beginning.

Plan ways of coping with potential losses. Consider what you would do if you suddenly had to fend for yourself, either alone or with the responsibility for an ill family member. Talk to each other about it. To sincerely hope that such a tragedy will not happen to you is normal and fine, but to behave as if it could never happen to you is foolish, particularly at a time in life when money is tight and your options may already be limited in other ways.

Loving and being close to other people always carries a risk—that you will be hurt or that you will have to cope with the loss of someone with whom you have shared your life and yourself. But the world would be a cold and lonely place indeed if no one took that risk. Good relationships are important in later life, just as they are at all other times. These relationships take work to build and maintain, but the return on your investment will be worth it.

Things to Think About

1. Relationships are important.
2. Good relationships take work.
3. You can plan for better relationships in later life.
4. Grief is finite: You can adjust to loss.
5. You can get help if you need it.

RELATIONSHIP WORKSHEET 9.1
Self-Assessment

Without discussing these questions, answer each one as honestly as you can. Do not consult with your partner. Compare and discuss your answers when you've finished.

1. In general, what kind of partnership do you have? 50-50? 60-40? 80-20? 100-0? Consider responsibilities such as decision making, taking care of social or emotional matters, financial planning, family organization, etc. If any area is designated almost exclusively to one partner, make a note of it.

2. Is this arrangement satisfactory to you? Why or why not? How would you change it if you could?

3. List five of your favorite things about the relationship.

4. List five things you would change about the relationship if you could.

5. List five of your favorite things about your partner.

6. List five things you would change about your partner if you could.

7. Go back to the first two questions. How do you think your partner will answer them? (Write them down—no fair not committing yourself to this one!)

8. Describe the two most troubled times in your relationship.

9. What were the three or four most important things that pulled you through those bad times? Name three or four things you tried that didn't work.

10. What would you say is the single largest hurdle you face when the two of you try to communicate? List three things you think would help.

When both of you have completely answered each question on this worksheet, make a date to talk about it, and follow the ground rules.

RELATIONSHIP WORKSHEET 9.2
Retirement

Without discussing these questions, answer each one as honestly as you can. Do not consult with your partner. Compare and discuss your answers when you've finished.

1. Do you and/or your partner want to retire? When? How?

2. Are you and your partner in agreement about whether or not, when, and how you plan to retire? If not, list three or four points of disagreement.

3. How do you plan to resolve these differences?

4. Have you had any worries about how well either of you will react to retirement? Explain why you are worried. (For example, have you noticed that you become unhappy or restless when you have a lot of time on your hands?)

5. Name and explain the three things that you are most looking forward to for yourself after you retire and for the relationship.

6. Name and explain the three things that worry you most about retirement, both for yourself and for the relationship.

7. For each of the following areas, describe the things you expect to change in your relationship if and when you retire:

   Time spent together. Do you envision spending more or less time together? Is that what you want? Have you talked about it?

   Household chores. If the house has been your workplace all these years, do you want your newly retired partner on your "turf"? Or are you looking forward to retirement yourself for sharing the chores and then doing other things together? What are your expectations if both of you are retiring from a job outside the home?

   Time spent with friends. Think about which friends you will probably continue to see after retirement. What about the others? How will you meet new people?

   Money. Consider how you manage your finances now. Do you both make the financial decisions? Do you both understand the budget, income, etc.? Do you provide financial support for your children or other family members? Can you continue this after retirement? Have you talked to these people about it?

(continued)

Time spent with other family. Do your children expect you to visit more often? keep the kids more often? Have you talked about it with them?

Where to live. Do you plan to move? Where? Why? Are you in agreement about it? Think about proximity to family, friends, health care. Would you be happy there if you were alone?

8. How do you expect to spend your time after retirement? List four things you expect to do more and four things you expect to do less.

9. Answer question 8 the way you think your partner will.

10. Overall, what effect do you think retirement will have on your relationship? Do you expect it to create problems? What are they? Name several ways you can think of to cope with them.

RELATIONSHIP WORKSHEET 9.3
Getting Older

Without discussing these questions, answer each one as honestly as you can. Do not consult with your partner. Compare and discuss your answers when you've finished.

1. When you were twenty, what did you think it would be like to be the age you are now? Is it as you thought it would be? Is it different? How?

2. Think back to when you and your partner first met. List five things that first attracted you to your partner. What do you think attracted your partner to you? (That's harder—list three!)

3. How has your relationship changed over the years? Think in terms of your emotional closeness and trust. Do you talk as often as you used to? do things together? take time to listen to and appreciate each other?

4. List three things you like better about your relationship now and three things you'd like to bring back from the past. Think of ways you could bring about these changes. (Make your suggestions as specific as possible. If, for example, you would like to feel closer to your partner, tell him or her that. Then propose that the two of you plan a vacation alone to a favorite place.)

5. Think about yourself, now or ten years from now. Are you worried about whether your spouse still finds you interesting and attractive? How do you feel about the changes in your body and your appearance?

6. Do the two of you still touch and hold hands? Are you satisfied with your sexual relationship? Can you talk about it?

7. What is your scariest fantasy about getting older? Are you afraid of getting sick? dying? being alone? How can your partner help you with these fears? by listening? sharing his or her own worries? helping you make plans?

8. Have you talked about how it would feel to lose the other to death or serious illness? Are there things you would want to say that you haven't said? (This is a hard thing for many people to talk about, but try to think of it as a gift of comfort you can give each other now. Sometimes it's easier to write things down than it is to say them.)

(continued)

138

9. Name two or three areas of your relationship that you handle almost exclusively now. Think about how your partner could handle them without you. Write down as many suggestions as you can for helping your partner to carry on. You probably know his or her weak spots better than anyone else does. Now's your chance to give as much advice as you like. Some ideas for your advice list: How to convert any financial assets you may have to cash, where the important papers are, how to keep social engagements going, what the secret ingredient is for your famous gumbo. These are serious matters, but you can have a little fun with it, too. Remember that the little things can be comforting in times of loss.

This worksheet will have you talking about sensitive subjects, so be especially gentle with each other. You may want to work through it the first time just getting used to some of the ideas and return to it at intervals throughout your later life, whenever you feel the need for a "tune-up."

Notes

1. R. J. Havighurst, J. M. A. Munnichs, B. L. Neugarten, and H. Thomas, eds., *Adjustment to Retirement: A Cross National Study* (New York: Van Gorcum & Co., 1969).

2. F. C. Pampel, *Social Change and the Aged: Recent Trends in the United States* (New York: Free Press, 1981).

3. L. P. Bradford and M. I. Bradford, *Retirement: Coping with Emotional Upheavals* (Chicago: Nelson-Hall, 1979). This is recommended reading.

10 Money

Money, which represents the prose of life and which is hardly spoken of in parlors without an apology, is in its effects and laws as beautiful as roses.

—*Ralph Waldo Emerson*

What to Know about Money in Later Life

Mrs. Miles was in the hospital after a desperate but unsuccessful suicide attempt. Her story unfolded as she told with shame and tears of the events that led to her trying to take her own life. Ten years before, her husband of thirty-three years had died suddenly of a heart attack, and in the time since she had maintained herself and their home by "making do" a lot. She worked some, got some help from her children, and received a small income from some investment property which her husband had always managed. At sixty-five she retired with a small pension and no savings. Then the property began to lose money, she had trouble finding part-time work, and she began to fall behind on her house payments. Finally, the investment property no longer could support its own taxes, and creditors began to hound her for her house payments and other bills. She did not understand the situation with the property, and it could be sold only at a further loss. When the house went into foreclosure, this healthy sixty-seven-year-old woman—an avid dancer and a hard worker with many friends—quietly made the decision to give up on life. She called no one. She went home, drank four glasses of wine, stabbed herself in the arm, and waited for death.

Mrs. Miles was not a stupid or an uneducated woman. She simply had not planned for any of the financial difficulties that befell her, and she did not know how to handle them. Her husband had been in charge of these things while he was alive, and there was little incentive for Mrs. Miles to learn about them and plan around them until it was already too late to make many changes. The situation overwhelmed her and she could see no way out.

Money Is Important

Having enough money is essential if your later life is to be rewarding and satisfying, rather than simply a struggle to survive. Your financial status must be considered throughout your plan. How much money you have influences, and is influenced by, physical and mental health, how you spend your time, and your relationships with other people.

Just a year before they plan to retire, an astounding 50 percent of people do not know what their income will be after they've stopped working. You can do better than that!

Most Older People Say
They Have Enough Money

In 1970, 25 percent of people over sixty-five were estimated to be living below the government-established poverty level. By 1983 the poverty rate was found to be only 3.3 percent. Why the big change in the figures? For one thing, Social Security benefits have risen more than twice as much as wages and salaries. For another, about two-thirds of older people pay no income tax. Nearly three-fourths of older "householders" own their own homes, and half of these have no mortgage.[1] In the United States over the past fifty years, for each successive group of older people, there has been continued economic growth, an improved standard of living, more widely available benefits, and a rising level of education. All these things have improved the relative economic lot of today's older population.

None of this negates the fact that many people, especially women and racial minorities, face severe economic hardship in later life. Another group that tends to suffer disproportionately is the "oldest old" (eighty-five and older), a population segment in which 21 percent are officially poor and many more on the verge of poverty.[2]

The point is, although there are inequities in our society for which we need to find solutions, you as an individual do not have to worry about becoming suddenly and mysteriously destitute when you reach a certain age. In one report, only 18 percent of older people said they "worried about money a lot," compared with 41 percent of younger people. For those in their later years, a lack of money was mostly a concern with regard to medical bills, and most of the older people found their incomes adequate to their needs.[3]

Assets and Liabilities

Where do most older people get their money? Social Security provides 39 percent, earnings 23 percent, income from assets 19 percent, private pensions 7 percent, government pensions 6 percent, and public assistance (such as welfare) 2 percent of the aggregate income for people sixty-five years old and older. Over half of people sixty-five and older get some money from savings and assets. Individual retirement accounts (IRAs) have become increasingly important in recent years, as government policies have changed to encourage financial planning for later life.[4] As you probably know, money you put into these accounts is not taxed until you take it out after you retire, when you may be in a lower tax bracket. Banks, which sell IRAs, will be happy to provide you with more information.

Financial assets and liabilities are not all measurable in dollars and cents. You are an individual, with monetary options and possibilities, not just problems to overcome. Thinking of yourself this way will help you to fight off any fatalistic, giving-up feelings about planning your finances in later life.

Personal circumstances that can be financially limiting include mandatory retirement and rigid attitudes toward the working older person. High medical bills or "iffy" health in yourself or a family member will require some extra planning. Heavy personal debt is an obvious disadvantage.

"Good as gold" personal assets include money management skills; a job with the possibility of gradually reducing the amount of time you work; a boss who believes in having good workers, regardless of age; and easily marketable skills or talents. Low expenses and supportive family and friends help. Energy and personal power are priceless.

What is the bottom line message in all of this? First, your planning can make a difference. You can maximize your assets and minimize your liabilities. You can take control of this area of your life. Having a certain set of financial problems guarantees neither successful nor unsuccessful financial adjustment. If the amount of money you have matches reasonably well with the things you need and want, adjustment is easier. If it doesn't, no matter what the cause—higher health care bills, expensive "wants" such as travel, the cost of starting a new business, inflation—you will have to plan more carefully.

Plan for Financial Health Individually

Remember what happened to Mrs. Miles, who was left with property to manage, but without the experience to do it properly? If you are making this plan with your spouse, both of you must be actively involved in the entire process. In many marriages, one spouse is primarily responsible for paying the bills, keeping track of expenses, setting the budget, and planning investments or savings. During later life, however, both partners must thoroughly understand the finances; either of you could be unexpectedly left alone.

Many people postpone or even avoid financial planning because it seems too hard. They feel that planning won't make any difference, or that they don't need to bother because they don't have a lot of money or a complicated investment portfolio. Some people just don't think about it, and others believe themselves incapable of doing it. All of this is nonsense.

The basics of managing your money do not require a degree in accounting, fancy formulas, or understanding difficult concepts. You've probably been doing it all your life. Unless you have especially large or complicated assets, keeping the income and the outgo in relative balance is about all there is to it.

However, there are some specific things to consider at this time of your life, and that is where the focus will be in the following sections. Don't listen to that little voice inside that says, "Oh, things will work out somehow. I don't need to plan." That little voice is in the minds of all those people who don't even know what their income will be after they retire. In fact, although it can seem like the most complicated area of all, thoughtful and thorough money planning can yield the most results for the least time and effort. Don't quit now—you're almost there!

Planning Your Money
for Later Life

What follows is a format for planning your later-life finances. In the Money Worksheets at the end of this chapter you will assess your current and postretirement financial picture, and get some ideas for increasing income and decreasing expenses. You will learn which questions to ask of bankers, employers, and the Social Security office. You will "practice" living on your postretirement budget.

Current Income and Expenses

Assuming you are still working, first evaluate your current financial assets and liabilities. If you have always been inclined to keep a careful budget, you will find this a fairly simple operation. If not, gather any receipts, deposit and withdrawal slips from the bank, and your canceled checks for the past year or two. You'll be using these to help you calculate current expenses and income. If you are doing this with a partner, note that Money Worksheet 10.1 has two columns, one for income generated by you and one for income generated by your partner. Do these Money Worksheets together!

Common expenses and sources of income are listed on these worksheets, but to make sure you haven't missed any expenses (or any income), carry a pocket-sized calendar for two months. Use one with enough space to jot down all your expenses every day. (Each partner must do this if there are two of you working together.) Each time you spend any money at all, write it down—item purchased and amount spent. Do the same for your income. This is an important "safety check." Underestimating expenses is all too easy when your income is good, but this is not the time to start fooling around with the facts about how much you spend for what. If you retire on a fixed income, you will be glad of the time you've spent now on accurate budgeting.

Income and Expenses after Retirement

The Money Worksheets at the end of this chapter are designed to help you predict your income and expenses after retirement. You will need to know what assets you have, how long you will have them, and how to be certain you can get at them when you need to. Using the worksheets, you will list your assets and note how to get the money out if and when you need it, which might require talking to your bankers, investment institutions, employers, and the Social Security office. It takes time, but there is a list of questions to help you. If you are working with a partner, both of you must understand your financial situation thoroughly. Remember the sad experience of Mrs Miles:

assets can become liabilities if you don't know how to manage them. The idea is to predict, as best you can, what will happen to each income and expense item if you retire.

Questions to Ask
about Your Assets

1. What assets do I have and how much are they worth? (See the Assets List on Worksheet 10.4 to be sure you've covered everything.)
2. When can I get the money?
3. Is there any penalty for early withdrawal?
4. If I lose my spouse, can I still get the money? Does it change the amount or the terms?
5. What if my spouse becomes physically or mentally disabled? Does that change anything? How can I transfer the assets into my name if this happens?
6. What is the tax situation for these funds?
7. Are there any conditions under which the value of any particular assets increase, decrease, or become unavailable to me?
8. What are the exact steps, and how long would it take, if I wanted to convert these assets to cash today?

Whether you are talking to a banker, an investment broker, a real estate agent, a personnel manager, or your boss, don't be timid about asking these questions. Ask them as many times and in as many different ways as necessary to enable you to thoroughly understand. Take notes during your conversations, and call these people back as many times as you need to. You are entitled to this information, and it is important that you have it.

Practice Living on Your
Predicted Retirement Income

If you are like most people, your income after retirement is about half of what it was before, and your expenses decrease to only about 70 to 80 percent of what they were when you were working. Can you live on your estimated postretirement income? You can find out by trying to live on this amount of money for two or three months.

Using your pocket budget calendar, keep track of the money you spend during these practice months, and compare the amounts to your postretirement expense estimates. Assuming that your usual income is higher than your projected postretirement income, try to put away the extra money (maybe in your IRA or savings account) so that it is not easily available. This will make your "practice run" as realistic as possible. If you find major discrepancies, go back through your budget and try again. Otherwise, congratulations! You have made a workable plan!

If you find that you cannot live on the amount of money you expect to have after you retire, you must start planning ways to increase your income and/or decrease your expenses. Money Worksheets 10.8 and 10.9 at the end of this chapter are designed to give you some ideas. Add your own thoughts in the margins.

Miscellaneous Topics— Wills, Where to Live, Crime and Cons

Wills

Everyone should have a will. Think about how you want any property or potential property (unexpected inheritance, for instance) distributed among your heirs. Without a will, the inheritance tax in many states may wipe out any assets, and the delay for your loved ones is unnecessary. Making a will is usually rather simple and inexpensive, so don't wait. See a lawyer and get it done.

When you make your will, communicate your wishes to the people involved. Henry Young didn't do that. When he remarried after his first wife died, he revised his will to leave his assets to his new wife. Unfortunately, however, he did not tell his children what he was doing. After Mr. Young died they were shocked to hear the provisions of his will, and they contested it. Court battles, heartache, and the destruction of previously cordial relationships between his loved ones were not what he wanted to leave behind. He just didn't think about what might happen. Finish your business so that someone else doesn't have to inherit it.

Where to Live

Where do you want to live in your later life? Geographic location, cost, proximity to friends, family, and medical care are a few of the variables to consider in making your decision. Don't forget to account simply for your own wishes. There is no point in doing the "right" or practical thing if it makes you unhappy.

Try to arrange to spend some time in any place you are thinking about living. This is particularly important for group living. For example, if you are considering a retirement community, think about whether residents have to be of a certain age. If so, will that be satisfactory to you or do you prefer a more heterogeneous neighborhood? Are there restrictions on who (what age) can visit and for how long? (Some retirement communities limit the visits of children.)

Consider carefully any move that would require you to put down large sums of money, usually for "lifetime" arrangements. Be sure there are no loopholes, and check to see if there is provision for full or partial refund if you change your mind later. Any major property agreement should be reviewed with a good lawyer. If you cannot afford full legal fees, you can usually find help by calling the local bar association or a low-cost legal services agency. The agency on aging in your area may also be able to give you a referral.

Think about whether you would want to live in the same place if your health changed. If you became disabled, would you still want or be able to live there? What about living there alone, should something happen to your partner?

Feeling "at home" in a place is an intangible. For many people, however, it is a very important intangible. Consider your own feelings about a place, along with all of the practical points. Where you live has meaning in your later life, so take time to think about it.

Crime and Cons

Older people are crime victims along with everyone else these days. Be careful of your personal safety. Lock your doors, have your keys ready when you walk out at night, and don't carry large sums of money with you. Police departments or other community service organizations may offer crime prevention or self-defense classes in your area. Such classes are worth taking to remind you of some basic prevention measures.

The number of con games used on older people is testament to the fact that the crooks out there certainly are aware of the increasing numbers of older people! The scams range from bogus investments or retirement plans to phony health cures. Keep in mind that if it sounds too good to be true, it probably is. Call the Better Business Bureau with any questions.

Coping with Financial Difficulty
in Later Life

Prevention is infinitely better than cure, but sometimes things do happen that are beyond your control. Bad things can happen to budgets in basically two ways—expenses go up or income goes down. Review Money Worksheets 10.8 and 10.9 for some ways to deal with unexpected changes in your financial status.

If you are unable to manage on your own, you may be eligible for public assistance such as Supplemental Security Income (SSI), welfare, food stamps, subsidized housing and energy costs, or Medicaid. Call the welfare office for more information. These are not pleasant things to think about, but many older people who need and are eligible for this kind of help do not get it because they are ashamed to ask. Try all of your other options. Then if you need the help, use it. That's why it's there.

Getting Help if You Need It

In setting up your financial plan for later life, you may find that you need professional advice from a lawyer, financial planner, banker, or tax accountant. If so, ask for the names of reputable people from employers, business people, or acquaintances whose opinion you value. When you have a few names, arrange to meet these people. It's important to trust and have a good rapport with anyone who is going to help you handle your money.

If your finances are not too complicated, remember that your employer may be able to help you with specific information about retirement income. Some companies provide their retiring employees with general financial planning help free of charge. If so, make use of it. Or your bank may offer such a service. Other lower-cost resources include the Social Security office and your area agency on aging. The latter can sometimes even help you find retired planners or accountants who know firsthand what you are facing and who do consulting on a volunteer, bartered, or low-fee basis. Beware of fancy courses and high price tags for any such service, especially if it promises more than information (i.e., How to Get Rich in Retirement While Doing Nothing). Such people *have* become rich while doing nothing, but at others' expense!

Money isn't everything, but it helps. That is true at all times, and later life is no exception. You can start now to plan for your financial health, and you don't have to be an accountant or a math whiz to do it. Money is a resource you can use to enhance the quality of your later life. Do what you can on your own, and get help if you need it.

MONEY WORKSHEET 10.1
Current Income

	Yours	Your Partner's
1. Income from work	_____	_____
2. Income from property	_____	_____
3. Income from investments	_____	_____
4. Savings accounts	_____	_____
5. Retirement accounts	_____	_____
6. Profit sharing and other employment benefits	_____	_____
7. Family contributions	_____	_____
8. Other income	_____	_____

Total current yearly income: Yours _____

Your partner's _____

Together _____

MONEY WORKSHEET 10.2
Current Expenses

First list your expenses in whatever way is easiest for you (weekly, monthly, etc.). Then go back and convert all to yearly amounts. (Multiply by 52 for weekly and 12 for monthly expenses.) Be sure to adjust for major infrequent expenses, such as tax payments. The list below is fairly comprehensive, but use your two-month budget calendar to make sure that you haven't missed anything. It's much easier to deal with forgotten income than forgotten expenses! Go through your receipts and your checkbooks to help you as well.

Per Year

1. **Home expenses**
   Rent
   Mortgage
   Maintenance (including furnishings and household
      supplies)
   Utility bills (gas and/or electricity)
   Telephone bills
   Home insurance
   Property taxes

2. **Transportation expenses**
   Car payment(s)
   Parking
   Gasoline and maintenance
   Car insurance
   Bus/cab fare

3. **Groceries**

4. **Medical and dental expenses**
   Doctor visits
   Dental care
   Medications (prescription and other)
   Health insurance (deductibles?)
   Life insurance
   Health maintenance (exercise class, etc.)

5. **Clothing** (purchases and maintenance)

(continued)

150

6. **Work expenses** (books, dues, classes, etc.)

7. **Income tax**

8. **Other tax** (self-employment tax, etc.)

9. **Other loan payments** (list all)

10. **Vacations/travel**

11. **Recreation** (movies, parties, restaurants, hobbies, etc.)

12. **Gifts**

13. **Financial assistance to others**

14. **Miscellaneous items from your budget calendar**

15. **When you have calculated your total yearly expenses, add 15 percent. That's how much most people underestimate their needs.**[5]

Total yearly expenses _____

MONEY WORKSHEET 10.3
Current Income and Expense Comparison

Total income from Money Worksheet 10.1 _____

Total expenses from Money Worksheet 10.2 _____

Assuming that your financial situation is relatively solvent at this point, the income and expense figures should be approximately equal. Ideally, you're putting something into savings. This is another check for the accuracy of your estimates. If your income and expenses are not compatible (assuming again that your current situation is relatively stable), there is a problem somewhere, and you will need to go back through the process again. Did you leave out one of your income sources? Did you underestimate some of your expenses? When your income approximates your outlay, you are ready to proceed.

MONEY WORKSHEET 10.4
Assets List

1. Savings

2. Checking

3. Stocks and bonds

4. Life insurance

5. Retirement fund

6. Business owned

7. Automobiles

8. Furniture and personal property

9. Other assets

MONEY WORKSHEET 10.5
Estimated Income after Retirement

	Yours	Your Partner's

1. Income from work

2. Income from property

3. Income from investments

4. Savings accounts

5. Retirement accounts

6. Profit sharing and other employee benefits

7. Family contributions

8. Other income (include Social Security and pensions)

Total yearly income estimated for after retirement:

Yours _____

Your partner's _____

Together _____

MONEY WORKSHEET 10.6
Estimated Expenses after Retirement

Per Year

1. **Home expenses**
   Rent
   Mortgage
   Maintenance (including furnishings and household supplies)
   Utility bills (gas and/or electricity)
   Telephone bills
   Home insurance
   Property taxes

2. **Transportation expenses**
   Car payment(s)
   Parking
   Gasoline and maintenance
   Car insurance
   Bus/cab fare

3. **Groceries**

4. **Medical and dental expenses**
   Doctor visits
   Dental care
   Medications (prescription and other)
   Health insurance (deductibles?)
   Life insurance
   Health maintenance (exercise class, etc.)

5. **Clothing** (purchases and maintenance)

6. **Work expenses** (books, dues, classes, etc.)

7. **Income tax**

8. **Other tax** (self-employment tax, etc.)

9. **Other loan payments** (list all)

10. **Vacations/travel**

11. **Recreation** (movies, parties, restaurants, hobbies, etc.)

12. **Gifts**

13. **Financial assistance to others**

14. **Miscellaneous items from your budget calendar**

15. **Add 15 percent to the total as before.**

                              Total yearly expenses
                              estimated after retirement _____

MONEY WORKSHEET 10.7

Estimated Income and Expenses
after Retirement

**Estimated yearly income after retirement
(Money Worksheet 10.4):**

Yours   _____

Your partner's _____

Together   _____

**Estimated yearly expenses after retirement
(Money Worksheet 10.5):**   _____

MONEY WORKSHEET 10.8
Ways to Increase Income

1. Work
Same job

Different job

Full-time

Part-time

Bartering (i.e., babysit for your grandchildren in return for housing, transportation, or food; trade your skill as a carpenter for your neighbor's help with your plumbing; paint your sister's house in return for the car she never uses.)

2. Retirement accounts and savings
Can you live on a little less now and put away more for your future? Calculate the difference between your anticipated income and your expenses after retirement. That way you can come up with a dollar amount per year that you need beyond what you have. Can you save that amount between now and the time you retire? (Of course, you will have to guess at how many years you'll need it.)

3. Investments
Discussion of this topic is beyond the scope of this book. However, unless you are already skilled in this area, you might want to get help from a financial planner. This kind of advice is fairly expensive but may well be worth the cost if you have substantial funds to invest.

MONEY WORKSHEET 10.9
Ways to Decrease Expenses

1. **Home expenses**
   Should you buy or rent a cheaper home?
   Can you make any major repairs or maintenance adjustments before you retire?
   Can you buy any major appliances or furnishings you know you'll need before you retire?
   Can you make your home more energy-efficient before you retire?

   If your home is paid for, you are at a distinct advantage and should think carefully, all other things being equal, before deciding to give up this significant financial asset. Rent or mortgage payments usually take 20–30 percent of income. Of course you have to consider taxes, insurance, and maintenance in making this decision, as well as any income you would gain. Just be sure to do your calculations carefully before you sell.

2. **Transportation expenses**
   Do you really need two cars?
   Can you pay them off before retirement?
   Do you need any major maintenance done now?

3. **Health insurance**
   Is yours adequate? (Get a reputable agent to help you assess this.)

4. **Loans**
   Can you pay off major loans and credit cards before you retire?

5. **Vacation and travel**
   Look into what is available in your area in the way of "senior" discounts. Newspapers sometimes carry ads from people who want to "network" their travel (i.e., you visit their home in Florida while they visit yours in Seattle). Such arrangements can help extend an already stretched budget to include some travel adventures, and you may make some new friends in the process.

6. **Money for your children**
   Can you afford to continue giving your children and/or grandchildren as much financial support as you have in the past? This is a sensitive area. *Talk* about it with them.

7. **Savings**
   Can you decrease your expenses now and put aside the money you save?

Notes

1. R. D. Hershey, Jr., "Modern myths about the Elderly" *New York Times,* sec. 2 (February 6, 1985).

2. Baltimore Longitudinal Study of Aging, 1958–present. As reported by Flora Davis: "How you can look and feel younger," *Ladies' Home Journal* (January 1986). G. F. Streib, J. Streib, and C. J. Schneider, *Retirement in American Society: Impact and Process,* (Ithaca and London: Cornell University Press, 1971). Also see note 1 above.

3. See note 2 above.

4. Final Report of the 1981 White House Conference on Aging, Department of Health and Human Services, Washington, DC, 20201 (1982).

5. R. N. Bolles, *What Color Is Your Parachute? 1985: A Practical Manual for Job Hunters and Career Changers,* rev. ed. (Berkeley, Calif.: Ten Speed Press, 1985). The 1993 edition of this book is recommended reading if you want to make a career change or go back to work after retirement.

Closing Remarks

In the world according to Freud, the prime directives of human life are to work and to love. Work in America has significance beyond simply the paycheck. People often derive self-esteem and a sense of identity from work. In such a context, retirement takes on significance beyond just a cut in pay. Because of the way our society is structured, this pivotal event called retirement takes place at a time when people are also adjusting to getting older.

In an ideal world, the activities of work, leisure, and education would be more uniformly spread throughout the life cycle. Currently, however, such is not the case. Retirement serves as an entry point into later life, a time of reassessment, change, and adaptation, a time of new growth and new rewards.

Our society has few well-defined roles for older people. Instead it offers two stereotypical extremes: (1) the person who retires to Florida for day after day of golf and sunshine, with few preparations and never a care, and (2) the person who retires one day and drops dead the next. The likelihood that you will fit either of these two categories is vanishingly small. You will not have a bed of roses without getting out there in the garden, nor will you be defeated automatically before you have begun. You can influence what happens in your later life by getting information and making plans—the goals of this book.

Anxiety about retirement and later life comes from uncertainty and the intangible effects of living in a society that no longer values age and experience as it once did. Planning decreases anxiety and increases concrete preparations—both of which are important to your satisfaction and well-being. Each new group of old people in this country is better educated and healthier, lives longer, and retires earlier. As the population ages and the ratio of workers to nonworkers changes, there are major implications for our society's productivity and ability to maintain the present system. Work and retirement policy should be more tailored to the individual, who should then be free to choose from a variety of work and life options, regardless of age.

The erroneous equation of retirement with aging and aging with illness, disability, and depression is distinctly without merit. For older people as well as younger, there is a spectrum of styles across a range of norms. What is important is that you are happy with your later life.

Employers and companies can help by getting rid of rigid retirement policies. Gradual retirement would provide gradual adjustment, continued use of training and skills, and more money for both worker and employer. Society can help by getting rid of retirement laws based solely on age and by providing incentives for the private sector to do the same. You must not allow yourself to be discounted on the basis of your age or work status.

Retirement and aging are interwoven, but they are not the same. Human beings are complex and so are their problems. Thus the focus of this book has been on the individual pursuit of later-life happiness. There is no single plan to fit all people, but you can assess yourself and make your own plan. This is not a scholarly piece, nor is it intended particularly as a social commentary. It is meant as a practical guide to help you prepare for a time in your life when many things are changing.

"The more things change, the more they stay the same." All cliches have a grain of truth, and the truth about later life is that how you coped with change before is likely to be how you do so later. This does *not* mean you cannot change, however. The stereotype of the older person as rigid and unable to change is just not true, although to change a long-established pattern you may have to work a little harder. Change—responding to the world and the people around you, growing with experience—is the essence of life. As long as you live you can change and grow. If your plan isn't working or doesn't suit you, start over and make another one. You are in charge of making this map for your own journey into later life. If you decide you want to go another route, you need only make a new map.

Congratulations on making your plan for later life. I hope you have learned something about yourself in the process. I expect your anxiety to decrease with preparation for both retirement and aging. Your self-esteem should rise as an older person with a right to personal fulfillment. Your expectations will be more realistic. But, of course, bits of knowledge laid end to end do not always pave the road to wisdom. I have asked you to question yourself and the world, to make and reconsider decisions, to think about difficult subjects. I hope you have come to know that sometimes things are not good or bad—just different. Your plan may not look like your neighbor's, but then you probably don't look much like your neighbor either.

I would like to hear from you—about how the plan worked for you, about things that could be improved or added, about how your later life is going. Write to me:

Deborah V. Gross, M.D.
100 Palm Avenue
Pass Christian, MS 39571

Thank you, and good luck!